from EVERLASTING *to* EVERLASTING

An abbreviated composite of spiritual insight as to how things work.

Robert E. Daley

The Larry Czerwonka Company
Hilo, Hawaiʻi

Copyright © 2013 by Robert E. Daley

All rights reserved. No part of this book may be reproduced or transmitted in any form or by any means without written permission from the author.

First Edition — October 2013

Published by: The Larry Czerwonka Company
Printed in the United States of America

ISBN: 0615875467
ISBN-13: 978-0615875460

Books by Robert E. Daley

A Case for "Threes"
A Simple Plan . . . of Immense Complexity
Armour, Weapons, And Warfare
From Everlasting to Everlasting
Killer Sex
Life or Death, Heaven or Hell, You Choose!
Raptures and Resurrections
Short Tales
So . . . What Happens to the Package?
Study and Interpretation of The Scriptures Made Simple
Surviving Destruction as A Human Being
The Gospel of John
The Gospel of John (Red Edition)
The League of The Immortals
The New Testament - Pauline Revelation
The New Testament - Pauline Revelation Companion
"The World That Then Was . . ." & The Genesis That Now Is . . .
What Color Are You?
What Makes A Christian Flaky?
What Really Happened to Judas Iscariot?
Who YOU Are in Christ . . . RIGHT NOW!

The Enhancement Series

#1 Book of Ecclesiastes
#2 Book of Daniel
#3 Book of Romans
#4 Book of Galatians
#5 Book of Hebrews

The Deeper Things of God Series

#1 The Personage of God
#2 The Personage of Man
#3 The Personage of Christ

Contents

Part One

Introduction 1

1. Before the Beginning 3
2. God Creates the Material Universe 9
3. God Creates Intelligent Moral Beings 13
4. The Probation of the First Social Order 17
5. The Judgment of the First Social Order 21
6. The Probation of the Second Social Order Begins 23
7. The Fall of Man 27
8. Fallen Angels Cohabitate with Human Women, Twice 29
9. God Enters Into a Blood Covenant With a Man, and the Jewish Nation of Israel is Begun 33
10. The Focus of Jewish Israel, and Why 37
11. Jewish Jesus of Nazareth Comes on The Scene 41
12. Jewish Jesus of Nazareth is Rejected and Murdered 45
13. Non-Jewish Jesus of Nazareth is Resurrected as the NEW CREATION Prototype 51
14. NEW CREATION Converts Actually Become a New Species of Human Being 53
15. The Super Natural Promise Fulfillment of the 21st Century: The Rapture 57
16. The Jewish Nation of Israel Comes Back to the *Front-Burner* of the Stove, and Seven Years of Prophecy are Finally Fulfilled 61
17. Antichrist is Dead, The Devil is Bound, and a 1,000 Year Reign Begins 65

Contents

18. Devil is Gone, Sinners are Judged, and the Heavenly City of New Jerusalem Descends From Heaven 67
19. Eternity Begins — What to Expect 71
20. Visions of the Future 75

Part Two

Angelic Social Order

Introduction 81
1. What Might Be the Possibility? 83
2. What Do the Scriptures Say About Angelic Individuals? 85
3. What is it That Angels Do? 89
4. Where is it That Angels Live? 105

Meet the Author 110
About the Cover 112

Part One

This is a short work, taking us from the point of origin in the Everlasting Past unto the launching point of the Everlasting Future.

The main focus is a step-back observation . . . from God's perspective on what is to occur during the 7,000 year, short work Probationary Period, for Mankind.

This Probationary Period, is a designated time allocation that the Apostle Paul refers to in the Book of Romans. **(Romans 9:28)**

Introduction

This short work is a brief summation of the things that have occurred from the dateless past, through the previous *Angelic Probationary Period*, into this current *Probationary Period for Mankind*, right on into the dateless future that lies out ahead.

This short work is designed to be informative concerning the one-and-only Living God, named "I AM THAT I AM."

This short work addresses the moral creation that exists within this universe right now, and attempts to give clarity as to who is who, and what is what.

This short work explains . . . in layman's terms . . . why God has done what He has done, and the reason that He has had to do it that way.

This short work reveals the part that the unique Nation of Israel plays within the scenario of the everlasting, and the various occurrences that have transpired on this Earth concerning that nation.

This short work will be formatted into a relaxed, Scripturally-notated, informal conversation between you and me.

It is our prayer that the information within this short work will be informative, enlightening, and possibly entertaining, for the average individual.

It is requested that brief consideration, at the very least, be given to what is presented here. The average Christian individual is woefully ignorant concerning spiritual issues of any depth, and the rest of the world, is as blind as a bat and is running headlong, at high speed, towards a cliff of everlasting destruction. Is anybody, anywhere, listening, or even interested? We shall see . . . won't we?

---

* all Bible quotes are from the King James Version

ONE

Before the Beginning

This chapter heading is certainly not normally what one would hear, is it? At the very least, the majority of Christian people on the planet are familiar with the idea of *In the Beginning* . . . but that is about as far back as it is usually hazarded to go. Anything prior to that normally would fall into the general category of . . . God . . . and that is all. And that, of course, would certainly be a correct summation, within its parameters. However, it would seem only logical that certain things that do not necessarily fall within the normal restrictions of measured *time*, most certainly must have taken place at some point.

The Scriptures, the Word of God, the Bible, is the only authoritative record that Human Beings have been given when it comes to issues such as these. God has purposed to give unto us all things that pertain to life and godliness *(II Peter 1:3)* so that we will be informed, and not be in-the-dark concerning important eternal matters. And so, it is to these records that we must go and draw our authority for any proposed postulations. Within the last thirty years, the gracious God of all creation has shared with this author, through His word, numerous *decisions and actions* that have occurred within the very council of the declared Three Persons in One God-Godhead. *(Romans 1:20; I John 5:7)*

* * *

First, since the Scriptures themselves confirm that there is only One God *(Deuteronomy 6:4; Isaiah 44:9)* but, additionally reveals that there are Three Persons that make up this One God, *(I John 5:7)* then there must be certain *decisions and actions* that have occurred between the Members of the Godhead so that there would be no schism, or division, or conflict within the midst of them. Ergo, there must have been a specific point in everlasting past when all Three Persons of the One God-Godhead, mutually and amicably, agreed as to who would sit within the position of, and be known as, the First Person, and who would fulfill the post of the Second Person's position, and who would then balance out the Trinity, within the position of the Third Person. *(Romans 1:20)*

Secondly, since the personage of God is not in any kind of wonderment, or at all befuddled as concerning who He is, but the members of the constituency of Mankind are most certainly able to become confused concerning Three-in-One, it is extremely important to establish and assign specific names and titles that would be ascribed to each of the Members of the Trinity for clarity. *(Romans 1:20)* These names and titles would then certainly be applicable in any of the dateless past *real-time* scenarios, as well as having a prophetical aspect for future complete-creative-plan fulfillment.

Thirdly, would be the question of assigned duties and responsibilities for each of the Persons. Since He is a God of order *(I Corinthians 14:40)* there must not be any possibility of cross-over conflicts that might gender confusion among either God or Man. The First Person of the Godhead should not find Himself in any conflict with the Second Person of the Godhead, nor with the Third Person of the Godhead in any matter having to do with original creation itself, or with creative operations, or with plans of reconciliation or redemption, when the time ultimately comes for them to come into play. This shall be effectively dealt with by mutually agreed upon authority and task assignments within all creative endeavors, and redemptive maneuvers.

The First Person shall be the head of, and administrator of, the existence realm of thought, *(Romans 1:20)* as well as the Most High God, *(Genesis 14:18)* as well as the Architect and Creator of all things, *(Isaiah 40:28)* and the future Father and God of the God/Man Jesus Christ of Nazareth. *(II Samuel 7:14; Ephesians 1:3)*

The Second Person of the Godhead shall be the head of, and administrator of, the existence realm of word, *(John 1:1; Romans 1:20)* as well as the Redeemer of Mankind, *(Genesis 3:15)* as well as the future Son of the Most High God, *(II Samuel 7:14; Psalm 2:7)* as well as the prototype and Father of the New Creation *(Isaiah 9:6)* and the High Priest of the Most High God forevermore, after the Order of Melchizedek. *(Hebrews 7:15-17)*

The Third Person of the Godhead shall be the head of, and administrator of, the existence realm of deed, *(Romans 1:20)* as well as the manifest power-portion of the Godhead, *(Genesis 1:2)* as well as the Comforter, *(John 16:7)* as well as the Spirit of Adoption for the future children of the Most High God, *(Romans 8:15)* and the assisting "I will never leave you nor forsake you" helper for the New Creation constituency. *(Hebrews 13:5)*

The Three Persons of the Trinity maintain their One-God projection and operation, by being absolutely harmonious within all three of the realms of existence.

What the First Person would think, the Second Person would also think, and the Third Person would not be any different. The fact that they would not necessarily think the same thing at the same time, does not diminish in any way their harmony.

What the Second Person would say, the Third Person would also say, and the First Person would not be any different. The fact that they do not necessarily say the same thing at the same time, does not diminish in any way their harmony.

What the Third Person can do, the First Person can also do, and the Second Person would operate no differently. The fact that they do not necessarily do the same thing at the same time, does not diminish their harmony in any respect.

That is why there is a need for amicably agreed upon duties and task assignments within the Trinity. Each of the members of the Godhead will meticulously remain within their operating parameters. There is no crossing over the line, ever!

Since the aspect of free-will-decision for all moral creation, shall be the center-most issue within the whole of the creation that God will be bringing forth, there is the distinct possibility of disobedience and rebellion. Any given moral creature that is granted a free will gives no personal guarantee that they shall choose to remain loyal to the benevolent Creator, and continue to be obedient. And since foreknowledge *(Isaiah 46:9-10)* is aware of the two major rebellions that shall indeed occur in the process of *time*, there needs to be the drafting of the details of two specific plans of reconciliation and redemption. *(Romans 3:24)* One plan is relegated to eternal, moral, triune beings, dwelling within Celestial or Terrestrial bodies (i.e., "Angels" and "Other Creatures") and the other plan is assigned to eternal, Express-Image, *(Genesis 1:26; Hebrews 1:3)* triune beings, that will dwell within Terrestrial bodies to begin with, and shall then transition into Spiritual bodies when the time comes. *(I Corinthians 15:40)*

When we understand that there are plans for restoration, that are to be established for the benefit of all of moral creation, then we should also understand that there needs to be a set of accurate records, that out of necessity, must be kept for *fairness* purposes. An accurate set of *books* is to be prepared to record all willfully disobedient and errant activities, that shall occur amongst all of the moral Human populous. *(Revelation 21:27)*

Additionally, a superior project of divine design that within the process of *time*, will actually deal with an unprecedented creation of a new-species of moral being, is drafted in liquid silver and dipped in transparent gold by the creative hand of predestination. *(Romans 8:29)* All of the details concerning this project are fully completed and in order, even before one second of created *time* ticks by. Everything having to do with this particular project is finished ahead of *time* because the whole of the project is accomplished by God, through the future God/Man, and for the benefit of the NEW CREATION new species constituents. *(I Peter 1:20)* Simple belief and acceptance of what God has done is the initial requirement. *(John 6:29)* Willful, continued obedience, and adherence to regulations will fully seal the *off the charts* benefits that go with this plan. *(Revelation 17:14)* And the entire basis of it all, is Love.

Finally, creation-regulation-restrictions, or the creative laws by which all things shall be brought forth into existence, and then operate continually by, need to be drafted, established, and installed. This includes the initial base set of laws (both spiritual and natural) and also whatsoever associate supportive laws that apply, that will work harmoniously and cooperatively with those base set of laws.

And with all of those necessary issues finally completed and locked-down, the created element of *time* can receive a green light to commence its operation. Within the corridor of calculated *time*, spoken thoughts are then uttered, Basic Creation Elements begin to interweave with established base laws, and the *things* of creation are then manufactured and manifested through the creative portal. *(John 1:3)* The Existence Program has now been started, and will travel on an irreversible path, into the trackless, limitless, eternity that looms inevitably ahead and defies comprehension.

TWO

God Creates the Material Universe

Everything has to have a start somewhere, and at some given point in *time*, does it not? Even secular atheists, it would seem, might have to agree on that particular notion.

According to the One who, at various given points in *time*, started all the things that are in existence, He is the self-declared Creator. *(Isaiah 44:8)*

The idea that there is no such being as the Almighty God, and that there is no intelligent life behind all of the creation, comes from the two-dimensional-thinking mindset of Man, influenced by death, sin, and Hell and is simply ludicrous at best. *(Psalm 14:1)*

God Himself declares that He does indeed exist, *(Isaiah 48:12)* and in direct contrast, many men of professed intelligence prefer to declare that God does not exist, but rather, that everything that is now in the state of existence is the result of some gigantic *Big Bang*. This author, however, challenges just who might be correct in their position?

But regardless of the expressed postulations of spiritual ignorance, the end result is a measurable, immeasurable universe filled with billions of immense galaxies that each contain billions of burning stars that potentially support innumerable solar systems, in which there are an untold number of planets of habitable conditions, capable of supporting life as we know it. And all of this universal activity did not simply *just happen* by *something* going BOOM!

For the sake of our short study, we are going to take the stated position that there **is** an intelligent, benevolent Creator who is behind all of this, and who has brought forth all that does exist, because of an incalculable Love. *(John 3:16-17)*

And with that as a basis, may we then understand that God possesses the unique quality of that which is called "foreknowledge:" that of knowing the end, or the completion of something, from the beginning. *(Isaiah 46:9-10)* And accordingly, He has drafted a plan for all of the inanimate material creation, and for the various creatures, both instinctive and moral, that are to be brought into manifest existence for the designed purpose of habitation of this expansive universal creation. *(Ephesians 1:11)*

* * *

We have seen that creative laws were established and ordained before the element of *time* began. And with the earliest of actions, Basic Creation Elements of Air, Water, and Soil, were brought forth and were infused with divine investment. These elements themselves would be the finished product of spoken-thought *(John 1:3)* and would be combined with other established laws of creation-operation and spoken-thought, to *create* those things that are seen. *(Hebrews 11:3)*

Without breaking any of the established laws by which all things have come into existence and operate by, God is then able to *hasten* His word in any given situation, and speed-up the very end result of the desired product. *(Psalm 147:15; Jeremiah 1:12)* Divinely spoken words, mixed with faith, and utilizing the three Basic Creation Elements, will produce whatever is precisely and accurately, described verbally in detail.

All of the material creation did not just *poof* into existence, as is so often put forth by Christian creationists who declare that *we see*. *(John 9:14)* And God said, "Let there be . . ." and POOF! there was . . . is not Scripturally sound, and does not even make much sense. Everything that is in operational existence today functions by a specific set of designated laws, not magic, and there is not one exception to that spiritual truth. So we will find that original creation, and the bringing forth of all *things*, is not going to be operating any differently than understandable functioning parameters. God is not a magician, He is a Creator.

And although the *time* factor is certainly an influencing criteria, this author does not agree that this universe is billions and billions of years old, no matter what the invented machines of Man indicate within their calculated measurements.

The length of *time* that it took to bring all things forth is not revealed unto us, even within the established reliable record of the Scriptures, but this author postulates that we are much closer to *the beginning* than even spiritual men today believe.

* * *

Upon completion of the material portion of creation, no matter how long it took, that included galaxies, stars, and planets; and on some of those various planets, mountains, seas, rivers, canyons, and extensive flora and fauna . . . the juncture is arrived at, that it is time to bring forth a moral creation for the benevolent pleasure fulfillment and satisfaction of the heart. This is not a creation of necessity based upon loneliness or boredom, but rather a creative expression of incalculable love. There is no need to creatively drag-our-feet, but there is also no real need to be in a hurry either . . . eternity is a long time. The size of the universe may be boggling to Man, but not so to the One who designed it. He has a Master Plan to merge size and purpose so that they blend together perfectly. And by His grace, an invitation has been extended to probational men, to be a viable part of this plan. A God of grace, desires to *share* what He is able to do, with any and all of the *whosoevers* of the moral creation, that are destined to be brought forth, and who would be willing to freely accept it.

THREE

God Creates Intelligent Moral Beings

Following our proposed *time-line*, we are now witness to a growing, expanding universe, that is void of any intelligent life, exempting of course, for the Creator Himself. And, by the way, the *expanding universe* notation is a scientific postulation and not a Biblical declaration. So a reasonable question would be, what specific uncreated area is the universe *expanding* into?

Solid Scriptural expose on these earliest of days, and of all of the creation endeavors of the Lord God Almighty are not prolifically abundant. The reason being, because they are not the spiritual focus of the *Plan* that God has drafted for the whole of the everlasting. However, spending focused time with God, coupled with an interest and an earnest desire for the truth, will be of much benefit concerning spiritual insight as to what has happened in days gone by.

When we finally reach the point of contemplating all of the aspects of intelligent life, we reach a juncture for an understanding of the whole reason for the creation of the universe in the first place.

And as Human Beings, we have been made privy, by the God of grace, to established reliable accounts of intelligent, moral, and free-willed creatures, other than Mankind, that occupy existence. *(Hebrews 1:13-14; Romans 8:39)* However, we do not have any further records, anywhere, from any other reliable source, concerning those beings who are referred to by the constituency of Mankind, as *aliens*. Once again, that is a postulation based upon an errant, active imagination.

What we do have is an informative basis for understanding the lower categories of intelligently created creatures. It is not arrogance, but rather fact that Man is in the highest of all of the *Created Creature* categories; and he is not here on this Earth by reason of the *evolutionary* process, but by the direct creative action of the God of Love. Man is noted as being brought forth into existence *in* the very image, and *after* the exact likeness of the Master Creator Himself. *(Genesis 1:26)* And as such, Man holds the highest position of all of the creative endeavors, within the whole of the universe. *(Hebrews 2:8)*

The two other distinct categories of *Created Creatures* would be the Angelic Hosts of heaven, and the Other Creatures *(Romans 8:39)* mentioned by the Apostle Paul in his letter to the church at Rome . . . whom at this time, certain un-named angelic beings might be ruling over (until the "New Creation Project" is complete) in certain of the focused universal locales. *(Isaiah 14:12-13; Jeremiah 4:23-26)*

Angelic Beings, of whatever ranking, would be inclusive within the second category of *Created Creatures* that God has brought forth into existence. Angels are not Human Beings that have *gone on* to become angels after their death, and are assigned the task of earning their wings by doing good deeds for Human Beings that are struggling through the issues of life on planet Earth. *Clarence* was still a Human Being, not an angel trying to earn his wings.

Angels are a distinct category of created beings unto themselves. They are indeed, spirit beings *(Hebrews 1:14)* that have a free-will. They have been gifted with intelligence, and supplied with a moral compass, and their essence dwells within a Celestial body. *(I Corinthians 15:40)* They have been brought forth in an *Eternal* state of existence, and have a capacity to live forever with God, if they continue in their obedience to Love. *(I John 4:8)* They vary in their appearance from *humanistic* to beyond a comprehendible description. Even though we may not have an understanding of the details, it is probable that they belong to a societal operation of some sort. It is unlikely that God would bring forth a creature that has no other purpose but focused servitude, 24/7, throughout an eternity of existence. That does not even make sense.

Angels vigorously participate in a myriad of activities beyond their societal involvement, within their service to God, and when Man is to be created, within their service to him as well. Angels are not precursors to demons. Demons are the spirit/soul residue of previous inhabitants of this particular planet. In their creative origin they were the first inhabitors of this planet, and they built cities, *(Jeremiah 4:26)* and formed themselves into nations. *(Isaiah 14:12)* Their physical death rendered them *disembodied*, and they are now referred to as *demons*.

FOUR

The Probation of the First Social Order

Although we know from Scriptural records that there was a First Social Order on this planet *(Genesis 1:2; Psalm 104:5-7; Isaiah 14:12-14; Jeremiah 4:23-26; Ezekiel 28:11-19; II Peter 3:5-7)* we do not know exactly when this society came forth, time wise.

As we reflect upon this Second Social Order that we now belong to, it is revealed unto us that God started all of humanity with one Man and one Woman. Natural multiplication over expired time eventually produced the teeming society that inhabits this planet Earth today. Biblical calculations are able to provide us with a solid, six-thousand year history of Mankind, but that is all. Every other postulation that is put forth is put forth by two-dimensional thinking, evolutionary men, who put their trust in other natural *evidence*, to calculate and substantiate their positions.

Might it be then that the First Social Order had proceeded along a similar path of travel as the Second? That is, begin with an original mating pair of creatures, and over a period of time obtain a bustling population? Or, was the plan to create an entire population, fully mature, without the privilege of procreative permission? We do not know the answer to that question at this time because we do not have any precise records to draw from. However, what is clear from the testimony of Scripture, is that whosoever or whatsoever these first moral creatures on planet Earth were, they were not Human. Mankind holds that unique *God-class* position, as being the only created creature to be brought forth *in* the image and *after* the likeness of the God of all creation Himself. *(Genesis 1:26)* What we do know is that these creatures eventually formed themselves into nations, *(Isaiah 14:12)* and excelled in building cities. *(Jeremiah 4:26)*

It would also Scripturally seem that this society was in need of provided governance and that there was, at that time, an angel in training that needed a task assignment that would solidify his obedience record. *(Ezekiel 28:15)* And so, the holy angel Lucifer was granted a throne *(Isaiah 14:13)* and placed within a governance position over the first inhabitants of planet Earth.

Sadly, we see that, with the intelligence that he was given, over a period of time the angel named Lucifer did not keep his thought-life in order, and his thinking began to go renegade. *(Ezekiel 28:17)* Within the capacity of his gifted free-will, he developed inappropriate personal desires, *(Isaiah 14:13-14)* and the end result, because of the anointing that he was entrusted with, and currently carried, *(Ezekiel 28:14)* by his actions there came forth the creation of a heinous new spiritual law within the universe called . . . the Law of Sin. *(Romans 8:2)*

We have no time records to inform us of how long Lucifer was in the governance position. Nor do we know how long it may have been from the time of the original bringing forth of the social order, to the installation of the governor. What we do know is that the Law of Sin snared Lucifer as its first captive, *(Romans 7:15-23)* and he began to slander God and lead his subjects down a pathway of eventual doom. *(Ezekiel 28:18)* In addition, Lucifer exercised influence over other angelic beings, and persuaded them to follow him in his attempted coup operations. *(Isaiah 14:13; Revelation 12:4)* When his preconceived assault to ensconce himself as supreme ruler, *(Isaiah 14:13)* was launched against the throne of God, he was soundly thwarted and was cast back down to his rebellious headquarters on Earth. *(Luke 10:18)* It was at this particular time, even though foreknowledge has been acutely aware of everything that has been going on, that God can no longer forestall the judgment that, of a necessity, must come forth.

Free-will, intelligent, moral creation has been brought forth into existence by a loving Creator of all that is, that they might have life and all of the blessings that a benevolent Creator would desire to grant. They have been placed into a position of subjection to a higher class being of creation, for their benefit of education and growth, and for the perfecting of his probationary training. An irreversible Law has emerged onto the scene as a result of unchecked iniquity, and that Law has effected a detrimental change in Lucifer's angelic-nature. And now, he is becoming the icon of pervasive, mounting evil amongst a fledgling society. Angelic associates operating in various locales within this universe, are being actively petitioned to join in with him in his seditious maneuvers, aimed at a God of grace, mercy, and love. Slander has succeeded in enlisting the subjective populous of planet Earth into agreeing with his evil rebellious proposals, and a crescendo of disobedience swells into an active assault, launched against the Holy City of God and the throne of Love. Forbearance reaches its limit, and action must now be taken to stem this tide of disruption before it goes any further. Needed judgment is about to occur. The whistle is blown, and the appointed lifeguard proclaims: "Alright, everybody out of the pool!"

FIVE

The Judgment of the First Social Order

The action of casting Lucifer back to his rebellious headquarters here on this planet, is followed by the *in-hot-pursuit* action of the God of Love, who will now turn His hat around, and operate as the God of judgment.

In much the same manner as sergeant stripes are stripped from the uniform of the now demoted private, Lucifer is relieved of the privileged anointing that he once carried, and his keys to the heavenly *executive washroom* are subsequently removed from his possession. His name is changed to Satan, to reflect the change that has taken place within his character and nature because of sin. He still has granted access to the receiving room of the universal Throne *(Job 1:6; Revelation 12:10)* but his associate angelic rebels do not enjoy that same privilege. They are severely restricted in their flight maneuvers, and are confined to the heavenly areas around planet Earth. They remain complete in the triune construction of their being, but they are eternally-spiritually-dead in their sins because of their refusal to take advantage of whatever catalyst that a God of mercy provided for errant eternal creations gone astray *(II Peter 3:9)* that they might be forgiven, and reconciled unto their Creator.

Attention is then turned towards the inhabitants of planet Earth itself. Cataclysmic natural events begin to unfold. Earthquakes in diverse places, *(Jeremiah 4:24)* all manner of chaotic devastation, *(Jeremiah 4:23)* the animal complement of the planet thrown into a panic and attempting to flee from destruction, *(Jeremiah 4:25)* the disseminating of the erected cities by earthquakes and planetary flooding, like that which will come about in the days of Noah *(Genesis 1:2; Psalm 104:5-7; Jeremiah 4:26)* and as a final judgmental act, light from the already existing sun, moon, and stars is withheld, and the planet is plunged into darkness as the Lord personally turns out the lights, leaves the scene, and returns to the Holy City headquarters of the universe. *(Jeremiah 4:23)* With the light turned off, and the subsequent heat that comes with it withheld, the planet quickly freezes and plummets into an Ice Age of undetermined length. All inhabitants, whether animal compliment or intelligent and moral, either drown or are destroyed by the freezing darkness. Their bodies being destroyed by decay, the now evil, intelligent, moral contingent of this planet become disembodied *demons*, and ultimately slave agents for the bidding of their wicked taskmaster, Satan.

Once the probationary activities are brought to a conclusion, a specific locale *(Deuteronomy 32:22; Matthew 25:41)* that we know of as the *Nether World*, is then prepared for the spiritual rebels to inhabit permanently.

The First Social Order on planet Earth is now a thing of the past. That which we know of as the *Angelic Probationary Period* is now a thing of the past. The leader of the rebellious insurgency has been removed from his governance position and judged concerning his disobedience and rebellion. His sentence is known, but it is not manifest as of yet. The sentences of his followers are known, but they are not executed as of yet either. Another Probationary Period lays directly ahead. Free-will decision, with manifested results of individual choice, has been determined. At this particular point in time then, let us bring forth our finest creation, and execute the beginning of the Second Probationary time-line. And in the process, we will purpose to definitively deal with the Law of Sin . . . forever.

SIX

The Probation of the Second Social Order Begins

In returning to the Earth, just as a person does when they enter into a dark room, the light, of necessity, must be turned back on. Genesis chapter one, verse three, is not a creative action, but rather a permissive statement. Whatever light-proof barrier that had been put into place with the judgmental actions of the Angelic Probation *(Jeremiah 4:23)* is now to be removed, and light from the already existing sun, moon, and stars is once again allowed to shine upon the Earth.

Because of judgmental consequences, certain issues need to be addressed, and *time* nuance adjustments will need to be made to the already existing sun, moon, and stars.

The total flooding actions of already existing waters *(Psalm 104:6)* and the absence of light shining upon the planet has caused the physical death of all moral creation, as well as the animal compliment and the planetary flora and fauna. So, it is necessary to separate the waters from the waters once again, cause the *sky* to be reformatted, bring forth portions of dry land, and then prepare to cause life once again to operate, within the planetary *dead-zone* of Earth.

The planet is spiritually pristine clean and has become physically habitable for a second time. *(Isaiah 45:18)* Trees, and bushes, and plants of all kinds are recreated, and a fully equipped special *testing* garden is even planted by the Lord Himself, in a particular location. *(Genesis 2:8)*

From the Soil and the Water, two of the three Basic Creation Elements, an animal compliment contingent for this Second Social Order, is brought forth. *(Genesis 1:20-2; 24-25)* Their purpose, even as with the First Social Order, will be for burden bearing, for companionship, and for food. And, at a given point in time, they will also be utilized for sacrificial purposes; that their life may become forfeit, and their innocent sin-free blood may be shed for atonement purposes, concerning a guilty, law-breaking Human Being.

The culmination of the creative process, results in an *in* our image, and *after* our likeness creation of an express image of the Creator Himself. *(Genesis 1:26)* Designed and activated in an unknown locale, the Man is then placed within the fully equipped special *testing* garden that the Lord Himself planted. *(Genesis 2:8)* Once there, the animal contingent is presented to him one by one that they may receive the *name-tags* that he would discretionarily ascribe to each one of them. *(Genesis 2:19-20)*

Disappointment that there were none like him, causes God to administer anesthesia and perform surgery upon Adam, to bring forth a complement for his personage. *(Genesis 2:21)* Bone of his bone, and flesh of his flesh, *(Genesis 2:23)* Adam *name-tags* her Womb-Man (Woman) because she came forth from him.

The Lord now has two exclusively special *creatures* that are original prototypes, of an entirely New God-class species of Creation. God purposes to put them in a position of ultimate authority, *(Genesis 1:28; Psalm 8:4-8; Hebrews 2:8)* extends His personal blessing upon them, directs them to become sexually active, *(Genesis 1:28)* and commissions them to fill-up, for the second time, the recently restored, sin affected, *planet-made-void*.

Adam is charged with maintaining the *garden* in an impeccable manner, and protecting the *garden* from assault by enemy forces. *(Genesis 2:15)* Sadly, at some early point in time, the enemy manages to seduce the most subtle of the beasts of the field *(Genesis 3:1)* and he in turn seduces the Woman, because of her lack of sufficient spiritual education from her tutor. *(I Timothy 2:14)*

When Adam does not correct her error, *(Numbers 30:6-8)* but rather follows her lead, *(Genesis 3:6)* the heinous, destructive and defiling Law of Sin is once again activated, and allowed to operate within the once cleansed planet, Earth. *(Romans 5:12)*

The serpent is challenged and judged, and relegated to crawl on the ground. *(Genesis 3:14)* The Woman falls from a place of equality with the Man and is placed in subjection to him, *(Genesis 3:16)* and the Man carries a curse with every thought that he thinks, or word that he speaks, or deed that he does. *(Genesis 3:17)* Together, Adam and Eve, and subsequently every Human Being that emanates forth from them, shall begin to sow Sin back into this world, thought by thought, word by word and deed by deed, until it becomes so overwhelming that something must be done. *(Genesis 6:5)* Because of the heinous effect of Sin, Adam and Eve are no longer *Eternal* in their design make-up. They have stepped across the threshold that separates the locales, and have become *Mortal*. And if they should be allowed or able to get back into the Garden of Eden, and partake of the Tree of Life, they will be able to live eternally, in a sinful condition. So, until the Tree of Life is able to be transplanted once again back into its original location, within God's city, the New Jerusalem, angels with a flaming sword are placed on guard duty at the Eastern gate. *(Genesis 3:24)*

SEVEN

The Fall of Man

When Adam was originally created he was of an unprecedented design. There were no other created creatures like him. There were indeed other moral creatures that had arms and legs and fingers and toes, yes, but that is not what we are talking about. Adam was God-class from his original creation. Adam was the only created creature that was an express image *(Hebrews 11:3)* of the Creator Himself.

When analyzing the personage of God, it is able to be determined that God has qualities about Himself that are *non-transferable* . . . these qualities belong only to God, and are not able to be transferred, even by Him, unto someone else. And there are qualities that God possesses that He is indeed able to *transfer* unto another creature, should He so choose to do so.

The *non-transferable* qualities are few in number:
1.) Self-existence from everlasting.
2.) Foreknowledge of the end, from the beginning.
3.) Omniscience.
4.) Omnipotence.
5.) Omnipresence.
6.) Light, Life, and Love in the absolute.

All of the other qualities that would make up the personage of God are able to be transferred at His discretion, and they are far too numerous to mention.

When God breathed into the nostrils of Adam the breath of life *(Genesis 2:7)* He transferred into His New Man, every single quality that He possesses (saving for the *non-transferables*) and the Man became a living spirit just like God Himself, who also is a living Spirit being. *(John 4:24)* On the inside, Adam was just like God. On the outside, Adam looked just like God . . . although at that point in time, none of the Members of the Godhead had any type of a body . . . they had only a *form (Philippians 2:6)* and a *shape, (John 5:37)* but none of the members had a body, until one was prepared for the Lord Jesus Christ. *(Colossians 2:9; Hebrews 10:5)* God and Adam were Father and son, by means of direct creation. And expectation was quite high on what the future held for them both.

Sin is a devastating Law, that was already in existence when Adam was brought forth. *(Genesis 2:17; Romans 6:23)* When Adam and Eve personally sinned, the acidic action of Sin caused the spirit of Man to become porous, and the spirit *life* that God had breathed into him, leaked out. When that occurred, the Man became spiritually dead, and became a living soul instead. *(Genesis 2:7)* It is not until the resurrection of the Lord Jesus Christ of Nazareth that spiritual re-birth and spiritual life becomes possible, *(John 3:3 & 5)* and any individual availing themselves of that gift, allows the living Spirit of God to enter into them, cause that the leaking porous action within their spirit is *sealed*, *(Ephesians 1:13; I John 3:9)* and the spirit of that individual is once again able to be filled with spirit life. That person, according to the Scriptures, literally passes from spiritual-death unto spiritual-life. *(I John 3:14)*

Concerning Adam, the fall from grace was devastating. He was triune in his original construct *(I Thessalonians 5:23)* and three-dimensional in his thinking processes. His choice to sin, and subsequent departure from the living God, dropped him into a two-dimensional mindset, and he no longer had the capacity of understanding things of an eternal nature and value. *(John 3:3)*

Because of Sin, physical sickness and disease was given license to operate amidst mankind.

Because of Sin, male and female equality was altered, and the *battle of the sexes* began. *(Genesis 3:16)*

Because of Sin, a curse became active and spread like a wild-fire upon the face of the planet. *(Genesis 3:17)*

Because of Sin, the entire progeny of Mankind was sold into slavery. *(Romans 5:12; 6:16)*

Because of Sin, Hell will be enlarged to accommodate more rebels than it was originally designed for, *(Isaiah 5:14; Matthew 25:41)* and those rebels will be coming from the God-class constituency of the universe.

These notations, and so many more, are the result of Adam disobeying God and falling from the position of grace from which he was originally created, and was residing in.

Now we are looking at the clean-up process that is going to have to take place, in order to get back to where the program was at the creation of God's express image *(Hebrews 11:3)* prototype.

EIGHT

Fallen Angels Cohabitate with Human Women, Twice

Angels were originally created a long time before men were created. Angels were created specifically for occupational servitude and ministration service. They were designed to serve God in whatever capacity that He desired them to, and they were to also serve God's express image creation, Man, when he is brought forth onto the scene. *(Hebrews 1:14)* Angels were allotted a specific time period for *probation*, to see if they were going to live up to all of the expectations that God had for them before God put them into permanent, eternal positions of responsibility. We do not have any type of a Scriptural notation as to how long that probationary period was.

During that *Angelic Probationary Period*, a specifically named holy angel, carrying the anointing of God, caused the Law of Sin to conceive and spring forth into existence *(Ezekiel 28:14-16)* That Law of Sin captured that angel named Lucifer, and literally compelled him unto all of the evil that we see within in his perverse activities. *(Romans 7:15-23)* Because the Creator of the universe is a God of love, this author is fully persuaded that a catalyst was provided, for the specific purpose of angelic reconciliation. *(II Peter 3:9)* Time and Scriptural record will bear out that the rebellious angelic populous and the subjects that Lucifer ruled over, refused to repent, chose to forego reconciliation, and have since become locked-down into an Eternal-Spiritual-Death condition within their poor decision obstinacy.

Since God is the One who gives His creatures their free will in the first place, using that free will to rebel against God will cause a forfeiture of that free-will usage when slavery is manifested within the kingdom of darkness. All of Satan's subjects are bound by his singular decisions and dictates. No free will is in operation by any of the subjects of the kingdom of darkness, whether those subjects be angelic or demonic.

Scripture reveals to us that at two separate intervals, fallen angels who, in appearance, looked like men, were sent by Satan to seduce and cohabitate with human women on planet Earth. *(Genesis 6:2; 6:4)* These angels very possibly presented themselves as *gods* to these women, in order to impress and seduce them, and to be able to produce unredeemable half-fallen-angel/half-human offspring who would be greater than regular men in physical power and might. *(II Peter 2:11)* Greek and Roman mythology, just to name two, are not just the product of someone's over-active imagination, after having pizza and a beer late one Saturday night . . . there is, in reality, a basis in fact.

The primary purpose behind sending these angelic agents would be to pollute and defile the pure human Adamic bloodline so that the promised Redeemer from Genesis 3:15 would not be able to come forth due to that bloodline defilement. Ultimately, neither one of those maneuvers were successful. But what you did obtain within the interims, was individuals from mythological backgrounds, such as Hercules (concerning the first sexual abomination), *(Genesis 6:2)* and Og, Bashan, and Goliath and his brothers, just to name a few (concerning the second sexual abomination). *(Genesis 6:4)* These individuals were *larger than life*, and obviously different from your average human male.

The consequence to these abominable actions, for the rebellious angels, was arrest and incarceration into the Tartarus compartment that we find within the *Nether World*. *(II Peter 2:4; Jude 6)* Bound with chains, they shall await the final decrees of eternal punishment.

[As a footnote: Do you honestly think that if the first constituency of these angels, that were arrested and incarcerated shortly after their immoral actions . . . was a known consequencial reality within the realm of the spirit . . . that you would be able to secure a second set of *volunteers* for yet a second attempt to thwart God in the same manner? This author does not at all think so. Again, this would present further evidence that there is no privilege of free-will operating within the kingdom of darkness. Residents within that kingdom must do what they are told to do, when they are told to do it.

When the ordained Messiah of God is born, there will be no further reason to sacrifice and waste valuable *agents* in trying to dilute the Adamic human bloodline. The deed is done, and we will now look to other ways and means, with which we may actively carry on this war.]

NINE

God Enters Into a Blood Covenant With a Man, and the Jewish Nation of Israel is Begun

Since the time of Adam and Eve's departure from His household, God has effectively been on the outside of Earth's activities looking in through the window. Adam was His righteous representative and agent in the Earth, and Adam's defection from God's employ and his new job of serving God's abject enemy, has left God with a situation. God no longer has any legal righteous representation on this planet, Earth. All human beings coming forth from the prototype couple are to become children of the devil by reason of inheritance. *(Romans 5:12; John 8:44)*

It is time to establish some righteous legalities to operate by. So, God approaches a pagan, Gentile, idolater named Abram, in order to offer him a legal-contract covenant *deal*. The basics of the offer are simple: "If you will allow Me to actively come back into this Earth to legally operate, through you, then I will protect you, and will provide for you, and will promote you, and will increase you . . . If you will but say *Yes*, then I will do all of the hard part that is necessary." The records testify that Abram chose to accept the *deal*, and at a point in time a Blood Covenant cutting ceremony was scheduled to take place.

Genesis chapter fifteen is probably one of the most grossly overlooked chapters within all of the Holy Scriptures. It is within this particular chapter that both major Blood Covenant contracts are established by God.

The first major Blood Covenant contract is confirmed between an infallible person named God and a fallible individual named Abram; and will include all of the other human persons that will come forth through his *promised* son Isaac, and his *purpose of election* grand-son named Jacob. *(Romans 9:8-13)* Because of the fallibility on the part of Abram, it is a covenant of credit, not of surety. *(Galatians 3:6; Hebrews 7:22)* Manifest covenant name-change causes Abram to become Abraham, and over a period of time causes God to become the God of Abraham . . . and then the God of Abraham and Isaac . . . and then the God of Abraham, Isaac, and Jacob. Within the covenant parameters, promises are made by God to Abraham, and specifically to Abraham's *seed*. *(Romans 4:16; 9:8-13; Galatians 3:16, 19, 29)* Due to fallibility on the part of Abraham's natural seed, at a point in time, a Law was given because of transgressions. *(Galatians 3:19)* Due to the reality of a *breach* that would occur concerning that Law, an animal-blood sacrificial system was established, and given as a *repair kit* to atone for the *breach* in the breaking of the Law and temporarily cover the transgression. And all of these, and a myriad of other nuances of the covenant pointed continually to the promised *perfect* that should come.

The second major Blood Covenant contract is established at the same time, but not ratified, between an infallible *smoking furnace* and an infallible *burning lamp*, and will include all of the other Human persons that will choose, in time, to become part of all of those who today are *in Christ*. *(Genesis 15:17)* Because of infallibility on the part of both the *smoking furnace* and the *burning lamp*, it is a covenant of surety. *(Hebrews 7:22)* Manifest covenant name-change causes God to become the Father, and all of the covenant Human Beings to become *Children of the Most High God*. *(I John 3:1)* Within the covenant parameters, promises are made by God to the promised *seed*. *(Galatians 3:29)* Due to infallibility on the part of both of the covenant participants, a Royal Law of love is decreed as a general guideline of operation, with no sacrificial system required, because of the final sacrifice that was made by Christ Jesus. *(Hebrews 9:26; 10:12; James 2:8)* And all of these, and a myriad of other covenant nuances confirm the promises that a loving God has made to *whosoever* would be willing to receive them.

A legal Blood Covenant is established on the Earth, and God has access once again to righteously operate with legality. And in addition,

Abraham becomes the first of a new type of Human Being. He is referred to as a Hebrew by the Spirit of Truth *(Genesis 14:13)* and as such, no longer belongs to the classification of Gentile. With Abraham and his wife Sarah, God now begins to build Himself a people. It is a slow process to start with, but it will grow to exponential proportions over expired time. The Nation of Israel is what they ultimately will be known as, and will be referenced to as *Jewish* both Scripturally and within all daily operations.

TEN

The Focus of Jewish Israel, and Why

Hopefully, for the purpose of clarity and understanding, this author will refer to the formation and development of the Jewish people as *"Project Israel."* And further, within the *cosmic kitchen* of the universe, this project is being attended to by God Himself and is on the *front-burner* of the stove.

To recap . . . right from the Garden of Eden, God Himself has a situation on His hands.

Because of the Man, Adam, the Law of Sin is operating within the Earth again. *(Romans 5:12)*

Because of the Man, Adam, all Human Beings are automatically going to be spiritually dead, because sin passes on through reproduction. *(Genesis 2:17; Romans 3:23; 5:12; 6:23)*

Because of the Man, Adam, God has no righteous representation on the Earth, and His hands are tied . . . at least for a period of time, concerning whatsoever He might desire to accomplish.

So . . . God needs to establish a righteous platform from which He is able to operate once again, and over a period of time, definitively deal with the Law of Sin, so that Human Beings may become spiritually alive once again. Thus:

The Blood Covenant that God enters into with Abram restores righteous representation in the Earth once again.

A re-confirmation of that same covenant, when the time comes, with Abraham's son Isaac establishes the legality and validity of *promise* operation and fulfillment. *(Romans 9:8)* Again, a re-confirmation of that same covenant, when the time comes, with Isaac's son Jacob establishes the legality and validity of *purpose of election* operation and fulfillment. *(Romans 9:11)*

Reproduction from the twelve sons of Jacob, over time, builds the number of Jewish individuals to exponential proportions while they are in Egypt.

Now, there is a two-million-individual plus in number nation, coming out of Egypt . . . and of necessity a law is given for the purpose of behavioral modification, called The Law of Moses. *(Galatians 3:19)*

In direct connection with the Law of Moses, an animal-blood sacrificial system is established as an effective *repair kit* for any *breach* of the established Law, in any aspect.

In the fullness of the time, the Second Person of the Godhead incarnates into the Man, Jesus Christ of Nazareth, and comes forth to rescue only the Nation of Israel from their bondage to sin. *(Galatians 4:4)*

In presenting himself to the nation as the promised Messiah, Jesus is rejected by the bulk of the leadership and is murdered in order to permanently deal with him, and remove him from the scene. *(John 1:11)*

Within the symbolic animal-blood sacrificial system parameters, Jesus becomes the genuine Lamb of God, and through crucifixion, is sacrificed on the altar of the cross of Calvary, being verbally placed there by the legally empowered high priest, Caiaphas. *(John 1:29; 18:14)*

Jesus is plunged into the abyss of darkness when he is made to be Sin, *(II Corinthians 5:21)* and subsequent to his spiritual and physical death, the unholy lord of wickedness is deluded into thinking that Evil has triumphed over Good and that he has won the battle at last. So, now ...

At This Point in *Real-Time* The 490 Year Prophetical Clock for The Nation of Israel, spoken of by Daniel the Prophet, Must Stop!!! *(Daniel 9:24)*

Project Israel must be removed from the cosmic *front-burner* of the stove, and placed onto the *back-burner* of the stove because the key person of the entire Project has been removed from the scene through death.

God has not cast away His people, which He foreknew, *(Romans 11:2)* but of necessity, they have temporarily been removed from the focus of the *front-burner* of the stove, and placed onto the *back-burner* of the stove to simmer, and to be provoked unto jealousy. *(Romans 11:11)* And this is why . . .

* The whole point of Abraham, was to produce the Nation of Israel.

* The whole point of the Nation of Israel, was to produce the promised Messiah, Jesus of Nazareth. *(Romans 15:8)*

* The whole point of Jesus of Nazareth, was to definitively deal with the Law of Sin through his death; and upon his resurrection, establish a new law of "Life in Christ Jesus." *(Romans 8:2)*

* The whole point of establishing a new law of "Life in Christ Jesus," is to provide spiritual life once again to any and all Human Beings that would be willing to receive it. *(John 3:5 & 16)*

And when the Nation of Israel, the Jewish people, the people of a Hebrew lineage, the Chosen People of God refused to receive Jesus of Nazareth as their promised Messiah, and the very One who came to rescue them . . . *(John 1:11; Matthew 10:6 & 15:24; Romans 15:8)*

Then, The Prophetic Clock Must Stop!!!

And, at this point in time, *Project Israel* can proceed no further. The *key* person of the whole of the *Project Israel* has been removed from the scene, and without the *key* person present on the planet, the project cannot continue, and must come to a halt.

God then purposes to start a New project that will be known as The Church, The Body of Christ, the "Project New Creation."

ELEVEN

Jewish Jesus of Nazareth Comes on The Scene

In coming out of Egypt, the Nation of Israel wanders in the wilderness of Sinai for forty years because of disobedience, stiffneckedness, and unbelief. *(Hebrews 3:17-19)* They extended an eleven-day journey into a four-decade sojourn because of their rebellion. At a point in time, all of the original contentious constituency dies off, and God is ready to bring His people into a land that He has prepared for them, that is overflowing in abundance.

The Book of Joshua in the Bible will explain unto us the difficulties that occurred within this transition from a wilderness wandering, to a milk and honey residence.

Once established in the land, the people begin to envy the nations around them, for whatever reason, and petition God for a king. The Nation of Israel was being ruled supernaturally by a Theocracy, but the sinful populous within the land clamored for the natural ruler ship of an earthly king. *(I Samuel 8:5)*

Granted with that king, the people soon learned that the fallibility of a sinful man was not going to be the answer to their desires.

Forty years of rebellion, followed by forty years of war, followed by forty years of peace brought the people no closer to God than at the beginning.

A divided kingdom sends the Northern tribes into captivity to the Assyrian Empire after the ruler ship of nineteen wicked kings. Eleven wicked kings and one wicked queen send the Southern tribes down the same path, but captivity to the Babylonian Empire was forestalled because of the ruler ship of eight righteous kings within the whole of the process. In both cases, idolatry and disobedience was many times the order of the day.

The ten Northern Tribes of Israel are never seen collectively again, but the two Southern Tribes of Judah return to the land once more, after a seventy-year captivity. *(Jeremiah 25:11-12)* They have seemingly learned their lesson concerning the worshiping of false gods, and because of that the active raising up of the prophets of God, for correction purposes, subsides and wanes out. Silence echoes from heaven for the next three-hundred years.

The supernatural birth *(Luke 1:18-20)* and raising up of John the Baptist gives an indication that God is once again moving on behalf of His people.

A decree straight from heaven, *(Luke 1:31)* the agreement of a young virgin girl, *(Luke 1:38)* and the overshadowing power of the Third Person of the Godhead, *(Luke 1:35)* causes an unprecedented incarnation to take place. *(Luke 1:35)* The Second Person of the Godhead, steps out of the locale of the Immortal, and into the locale of the Eternal, in order to put on a suit of flesh and become the Man, Jewish Jesus of Nazareth. *(Hebrews 2:14; 10:5)*

As difficult as it is for most people to believe, for the first twelve-years of his life, this young man does not really know who he is. *(Luke 2:49; Philippians 2:8)* From the moment of revelation recognition, his life dramatically changes *(Luke 2:49)* and eighteen-years of Scriptural silence immediately follow.

At the age of thirty *(Luke 3:23)* Jewish Jesus is unctioned by the Holy Spirit of God to travel down from the northern town of Nazareth to the Jordan River in the south, in order to present himself unto the only ordained prophet of God that was on the scene. Through water baptism, God reveals unto John who the Messiah for the Nation of Israel is, *(Amos 3:7; Matthew 3:14; John 1:33)* and John proclaims to the people that he ministers to that the Promised One is now on the scene and in their midst. *(John 1:26)*

Immediately following his water baptism, Jewish Jesus of Nazareth is unctioned to retire into the wilderness *(Mark 1:12)* for six weeks, in order to submit himself therefore unto God and resist the devil, *(James 4:7)* and to *tune-in* to the still small voice of the Spirit of Grace. *(I Kings 19:11-12)* Preparation for public ministry is the reason for the journey and is what is in active manifestation, concerning this wilderness ordeal.

A serious study of the Gospels will bear out that all of the public ministration that occurred through Jewish Jesus of Nazareth was accomplished by the active operation of the Gifts of the Holy Spirit that we find expounded upon by the Apostle Paul within the Book of I Corinthians. *(I Corinthians 12:4-11)* Everything that Jesus did, he did as a man, and everything that Jesus did as a man, he did as a man sensitive to, and submitted to, the direction of the Holy Spirit of God. And at the conclusion of his ministry, Jewish Jesus turned right around and told his Jewish disciples that they would be able to do the same things that he had done. *(John 14:12)*

Discernment of what is taking place will also reveal that the Kingdom of Heaven is proclaimed and offered unto the Nation of Israel. *(Matthew 4:17)* That presentation is followed closely by the presenting of the King that is slated to rule that kingdom. *(Isaiah 9:6-7; Matthew 2:6)*

For several years Jewish Jesus of Nazareth crisscrossed the land of Israel ministering healing and deliverance, and God's reconciling love unto the occupied covenant people of the living God. However, abject hatred and jealously of the sinless prophesied man *(Hebrews 4:15)* religiously refuses the offered kingdom, and finally, focused attention and purpose of will, manifests murder as the solution to this troubling situation. *(John 11:49-50)*

TWELVE

Jewish Jesus of Nazareth is Rejected and Murdered: Focus of the Jewish Nation of Israel Moves to the *Back-Burner* of the stove

* From before the beginning, the Nation of Israel is not intended to be the whole probationary picture that we are looking at. It is, in fact, only going to be one piece of the ultimately completed puzzle. And even though it is an important piece to be sure, it is not the most significant piece within the whole of the portrait. *

Jewish Jesus of Nazareth was a bold man, in the natural. Jewish Jesus of Nazareth was a courageous man amidst manifested fear. Some people considered Jewish Jesus of Nazareth to be an upstart, and a rebel, and a rogue. But in reality, Jewish Jesus of Nazareth was the one and only perfect human being that ever was, or is, or ever will be. *(John 8:29; 14:30)* He ministered to various kinds of people without ever allowing himself to become intimidated.

But, when Jewish Jesus of Nazareth raised up Mary and Martha's brother Lazarus from the dead, it was the last straw. He had, in fact, raised up other people from the dead along the ministerial road, but the raising up of Lazarus was a much more public event than any of the others. The Pharisees and the Sadducees could not let this pass. They potentially thought, "If he is allowed to continue, there will be no stopping him . . . he will be able to do anything." So, he must be stopped, even if it requires collusion with the governmental occupying forces of Rome.

The Triumphal Entry into Jerusalem was the beginning of the end for the God/Man, Jewish Jesus of Nazareth, concerning his time on this Earth. *(Matthew 21:8-11)* With the recent raising of Lazarus from the dead, the general public is rejoicing and exuberant concerning this affirmed prophet of the Lord. The celebrating multitudes receive him as the One to come, but the majority of the religious leadership demonstrate contempt and jealousy.

During most of his final week, before his death, Jesus ministered and taught during the day-time within the city of Jerusalem, but in the evening he went to Lazarus' home.

Judas Iscariot, at this point, is fully into his agenda of attempting to force Jesus' hand to move against the Roman occupiers with the power that he has demonstrated on so many occasions. The Pharisees, catching wind of Judas' intentions, financially seduce him into betraying the Lord of Glory. *(Luke 22:4-5)* At the Last Supper, Jesus repeatedly attempts to warn Judas of the impending danger that lies directly ahead, but Judas is not listening. *(Matthew 26:23-24; Luke 22:22)* Scripture reveals that after his departure from the table, Jesus prayed for the remaining disciples. *(John 17:9)* At a point in time, Jesus specifically prayed for Peter. *(Luke 22:31-32)* And by the grace of God, Jesus prayed for you and me, even though we are not due to come onto the scene for hundreds and hundreds of years. *(John 17:20)* But what is sadly absent from the Scriptural records, is any petition or prayer that might have been offered on behalf of Judas Iscariot. Jesus purposely did not cover Judas with prayer protection because of foreknowledge of what was to come; including knowledge that, over a period of time, Judas would be swallowed up through the spirit of heaviness with overmuch sorrow, and ultimately commit suicide. *(II Corinthians 2:7)* Since God is not willing that any moral being should perish, *(II Peter 3:9)* not even an individual like Judas Iscariot, we need to re-adjust our thinking, especially when it comes to even the most heinous of persons.

Betrayal within a garden of prayer *(Luke 22:48)* brings Jewish Jesus before the biased *judges* of the court of the Sanhedrin. Condemnation from them, *(Mark 14:63-64)* and exerted allegiance pressure upon Pontius Pilate from the people who hated Jewish Jesus, *(John 19:12)* results in the issuance of a death sentence, to be carried out by the heinous means of Roman crucifixion.

Upon the utterance of the fifth out of seven statements that Jesus makes from the cross of Calvary, *(John 19:28)* Scriptural alignment and fulfillment up unto this precise moment in real time is fully complete, the tide of the occurring events has become irreversible . . . and Jesus declares **"IT IS FINISHED"**, *(John 19:30)* concerning his Scriptural obligations and God's first-part dealings of the Abrahamic Covenant, with the Nation of Israel.

The statement that Jewish Jesus of Nazareth has just uttered, has nothing whatsoever to do with the *Plan of Redemption* as is put forth by so many within Christianity. There is, in fact, no such thing as *Christianity* even in existence at this point in real time.

It is eternally important that we understand what actually took place, concerning both of the deaths of Jewish Jesus of Nazareth. Our personal forever and ever may depend upon it. *(John 3:3; 3:5)* As Man is made up of three portions in his compositional construct, *(I Thessalonians 5:23)* and as Jewish Jesus of Nazareth was fully a Man, *(Hebrews 2:14; 2:17)* we should have a working knowledge of what actually happened, Scripturally, to each of those portions of Jewish Jesus of Nazareth when he experienced both a spiritual and a physical death. Working from the outside to the inside:

#1 The portion of his being, which was a Terrestrial/physical body, was offered in a sacrificial manner to fulfill and pay for mandatory indebtedness for what the Law of Sin's full effect is on the physical portion of any Man. *(Hebrews 10:9-10; Isaiah 53:4-5; I Peter 2:24)*

#2 The portion of his being, which was his soul, consisting of his intellect, emotions, and free-will, was bruised and grieved as it was offered in a sacrificial manner, to fulfill and actually pay for the ultimate indebtedness of what the Law of Sin's ravaging and devastating effect is on the free-will of God's most precious creation. *(Isaiah 53:10; Romans 7:15-23)*

#3 The portion of his being, which is the real epicenter of every Man, that is his spirit, was actually made to be Sin *(II Corinthians 5:21)* so that the crushing power of spiritual-death upon Man would be stayed and definitively halted in its tracks. The Second Person of the Godhead, the God/Man, Jewish Jesus of Nazareth literally succumbed to spiritual-death in order to fulfill and pay for the indebtedness that the Law of Sin demands and extracts from every one of its captives. *(Genesis 2:17; Romans 5:12; 6:23; Hebrews 2:9)*

Jewish Jesus of Nazareth did not do all of these things for himself. Rather, because, as the Second Person of the Godhead, He is the one that created Man, *(Genesis 1:26; John 1:1)* He is fully able when the time comes, *(Galatians 4:4)* and He becomes a Man Himself, *(John 1:14; Hebrews 2:14; 2:17)* to stand in the position of representation for all other men, everywhere. And as a species representative, whatsoever he experiences and accomplishes personally, shall be extended to all individuals who would be willing to accept his representation.

As the Second Person of the Godhead, He **is** Light, *(I John 1:5)* and He **is** Love, *(I John 4:8)* and He **is** Life. *(John 14:6; I John 1:2; 5:11-12; 20)* Who you **is**, and what you **has**, even though it is grammatically incorrect, are two different things. So, the reality of the matter is that the self-existent, unchanging *Life* aspect of the Second Person of the Godhead, in the human person of Jewish Jesus of Nazareth, was swallowed up by death. And, the self-existent, unchanging *Light* aspect of the Second Person of the Godhead, in the human person of Jewish Jesus of Nazareth, was snuffed out by darkness. But the self-existent, unchanging *Love* aspect of the Second Person of the Godhead, in the human person of Jewish Jesus of Nazareth, remained untouched by Sin and fully intact, and prevailed throughout the entire crucifixion and death process. *(I Corinthians 13:8; 13:13; Hebrews 13:8)* And ultimately, that is what carried the testator of the entire universe of God's creation, from one side of the cross to the other *(Hebrews 9:16-17)* just as the Scripture says. *(I Corinthians 13:8)*

With the death of Jewish Jesus of Nazareth, God's focused attention is no longer on the Hebrew, Chosen People of God, Nation of Israel. The builders have rejected the stone, *(Matthew 21:42; Ephesians 2:20; I Peter 2:6-7)* and God has honored their decision as it falls into the acceptable aspect of His one will. *(Romans 12:2)* He has not cast them away, *(Romans 11:2)* but He has moved them to the *back-burner* of the cosmic stove in order for them to simmer. They were first offered the privilege of being the supreme constituency of Humanity. Now, after the probation is complete, they will occupy the superior position of natural man. God will now shift His attention and focus, and will in fact, begin a New *Project*. Heavenly excitement is high as we reach the precipice of the most momentous *event* that universal history shall ever witness.

THIRTEEN

Non-Jewish Jesus of Nazareth is Resurrected as the NEW CREATION Prototype

Elements of sinless humanity lay silently within the guarded sepulcher. *(Matthew 28:2-4; II Corinthians 5:21)* The Scriptural *time* factor is only seconds from expiration. *(Matthew 12:40)* Prophetical declarations from a word that is settled in heaven forever, *(Psalm 119:89)* and has been collected from centuries past, have now been gathered together for the purpose of creation-merging. And when the last second of a seventy-two hour time decree reaches the point of reality *(Matthew 12:40; 27:63; Mark 8:31; John 2:19)* those prophetical declarations are supernaturally infused into that sinless body, in line with the legalities of a newly established law, *(Romans 8:2)* and a creative, super-nova, spiritual explosion, occurs by the power of the Third Person, Holy Spirit of God *(Romans 8:11)* as an unprecedented NEW CREATION Human Being is birthed forth into existence. *(II Samuel 7:14; Psalm 2:7; Acts 13:33; Colossians 1:15; 18; Revelation 3:14)* This One will WOW! the crowd.

Everything about this Man, Jesus Christ of Nazareth, is now BRAND NEW! He **is** still the same person that he has always been, *(Hebrews 13:8)* but now he is also different. He was, and is, the Second Person of the Godhead from everlasting. When incarnation occurred, He became the Second Person-God/Man, Jewish Jesus of Nazareth. When he was raised up from the spiritual and physical dead, he became the Second Person-God/Man, New Creation Jesus of Nazareth. He is a Prototype of something BRAND NEW! He does not live within either the Eternal or Mortal locales of existence anymore, because he has accomplished the task that he was assigned, and has become an Immortal person once again. *(I Corinthians 15:53; II Timothy 1:10)* Because of that immortality he is no longer on the natural level, but has become supernatural in his personage; and has extended an invitation for *whosoever* to join him in also becoming supernatural; and in addition, also one of the immortals. *(John 3:16; I Corinthians 15:53)* He is not a Jewish man anymore, which seems to be an upset to so many Christians when that truth is revealed, because he is a New Creation creature now, in which there is no Jew, and there is no Gentile. *(I Corinthians 12:13; Galatians 3:26-28)* And, now that he has become a New Man he has broken down the middle wall of partition that used to exist between the natural Jew and the natural Gentile, for those that find themselves part of the reality of being *in Christ*. *(Ephesians 2:14)* He has secured the keys of death and hell, by his triumph over Sin and death, *(Colossians 1:13; Revelation 1:18)* and faith in him delivers us from the power of darkness, and translates us into the kingdom of God's dear Son. He has become the testator *(Hebrews 1:2; 9:16-17)* of the Second Covenant, *(Hebrews 10:9)* which is actually the heart of the New Testament. He sits in a position of authority at the very right hand of the Almighty God of the universe, *(Ephesians 1:20; Hebrews 2:8-9)* and shall temporarily reign over the Nation of Israel for 1,000 years *(Isaiah 9:6; Revelation 20)* on this Earth. At the conclusion of the 1,000 years, Jesus will turn over the active reigning scepter of authority, concerning the Nation of Israel, to the resurrected, New Creation, King David, to whom the throne of monarchy was promised in the first place. *(Ezekiel 37:20-28)* He will then prostrate himself before the Father in heaven, and present unto Him the finished work that he was assigned to accomplish, *(I Corinthians 15:24-28)* from *before the beginning.*

He is now the golden die from which the silver coins of divine childhood shall be cast, *(I John 3:1)* and the extensive span of forever is found incarnate within him.

FOURTEEN

NEW CREATION Converts Actually Become a New Species of Human Being

"And when he had said this, he breathed on them, and saith unto them, Receive ye the Holy Ghost:"
(John 20:22)

This is the reality of where it all starts for this New Creation Project that is launched forth by Almighty God the Father.

After a new product has been ideally, mentally, conceived and then converted into a mechanical drawing, the next step in the process is to produce the first . . . and only . . . prototype. That initial prototype is then thoroughly tested, and upon creator-approval, the order is given to move the factory into high-gear, start the assembly line, and begin the mass production of this new space-age, innovative, miracle product.

The New Creation Project runs along that same line of process. The idea-conception occurred within the infinite mind of the Godhead, during the expanse of the everlasting past. The mechanical drawing was, in reality, manifest as chosen words of spoken-thought *(John 1:1-3)* that were uttered forth by the Second Person of the Godhead. The actual creation of the prototype was a unified corporate effort of all Three Members of the Godhead Trinity, within each of Their specific operating capacities. *(Genesis 1:26)* And, the thorough testing process began within a garden setting, and was finally completed 4,000 years later with a perfect subject named Jewish Jesus of Nazareth.

The person of Jesus of Nazareth was, and is, God manifest in the flesh, that is true. *(I Timothy 3:16)* However, he is also 100% Man, *(Hebrews 2:14; 17)* and it is the huMANity portion of Jesus that we need to put our focus upon, as being the ultimate created product of the Divine mind.

Once again, we need to understand that fore-knowledge *(Isaiah 46:10)* was acutely aware of the heinous destruction that the Law of Sin would bring into existence, and the extensive rip that it would affect within the harmonious tapestry of the created universe. And if that Law of Sin is left un-dealt with, there would never be an opportunity to return to a continuum of the blissful original universal harmony that once was. Therefore:

* The ultimate reason and original purpose for the creation of planet Earth was to provide a suitable testing ground for the Express Image creation of the Most High God. *(Hebrews 1:3)*

* The ultimate reason and original purpose for the Abrahamic Blood Covenant and the creation of the Nation of Israel was to re-establish the lost righteous representation within the God-class constituency of this Earth, known as Humanity.

* The ultimate reason and special purpose for Jewish Jesus of Nazareth is two-fold: First and foremost, is to provide a legal sacrifice that can definitively deal with the heinous Law of Sin, by utilizing a personal, sacrificial partaking, of the very Law itself, and the death-condition that the Law of Sin produces. *(II Corinthians 5:21; Hebrews 2:9)* And secondly, to complete and ratify the garden-setting-product-testing process, while fulfilling the Blood Covenant promises that were made, at the same time. *(Romans 15:8)*

Now that those two goals have been obtained, it is time to go on unto perfection. *(Hebrews 6:1)* The unprecedented work of the NEW CREATION, is nothing less than universe-altering, and is the genesis of a brand new species of Human Being that has never existed before the resurrection of the New Creation-Jesus of Nazareth.

NEW does not mean a re-working or a remodeling of the Old. NEW does not mean establishing compatibility and a homogenizing with the Old. NEW means NEW. Old is completely gone, and all things are become NEW. *(II Corinthians 5:17-18)* Even time calculation has been altered since that event took place—2,015 years from what?

As difficult as it is to grasp (and please trust this author when he says that it seems to be extremely difficult for most people to wrap their brains around) the resurrection of the New Creation Jesus of Nazareth is the very beginning of a NEW SPECIES of Human creation. Just like there were no creatures called *people* anywhere within the entire universe before Adam was created . . . so there were no *New Creation* individuals before New Creation Jesus of Nazareth was resurrected from the dead. He is the one that started the whole thing.

All of the essential workings that may be included, and available, within the finished work of the New Creation Christ Jesus, operate and function by faith. And, those workings are, in reality, activated by the process of personally believing. Identification with Christ is established by faith, and activated by personal believing. *(Ephesians 1:1)* Being seated at the right hand of God the Father is established by faith, and activated by personal believing. *(Ephesians 1:20)* Being more than a conqueror is established by faith, and activated by personal believing. *(Romans 8:37)* Being delivered from the powers of darkness, and translated into the kingdom of God's dear son, is established by faith, and activated by personal believing. *(Colossians 1:13)* Even our being begotten from above is established by faith, *(John 1:12; Ephesians 2:8)* and activated by personal believing. *(Romans 10:10)* So, understand that all of the spiritual realities of the New Creation resurrection, are legally and firmly established by the faith of the New Creation Jesus of Nazareth himself, *(John 1:12; Ephesians 2:8; Galatians 2:20)* and activated by each and every individual that chooses to receive what God has freely provided, through personal believing.

When the disciples were breathed upon by the New Creation Jesus of Nazareth, *(John 20:22)* there was an impartation of spiritual power that passed, within his very breath, from the resurrected Lord of Glory into those cleansed vessels of honor. *(John 15:3; II Timothy 2:21)* They became born-again *(John 3:3; 5)* right then and there, and were not even consciously aware of what had happened. New Creation Jesus' breathing upon them was an initiating act of God, concerning the new species of Human Being, of which New Creation Jesus of Nazareth was the prototype and original product. And now, the first divine coins of silver, have just left the die.

During the following six weeks, the New Creation Jesus visibly appears several times, and at various places, before as many as five hundred people at one time. *(I Corinthians 15:5-7)* At his final appearance, before returning to heaven, he gave specific instructions for his New Creation believing followers to fulfill. *(Acts 1:4-8)*

By the time that the Day of Pentecost was fully come, *(Acts 2:1)* there were less than one hundred and fifty born-again, recreated, seated at the right hand of the Father, new species, New Creation believers in existence. The resurrection realities are being manifest through personal testimonies and times of sharing by new believers, but the bulk of the flock of Israel are still dead in their sins. The Feast of Pentecost saw three thousand new species conversions unto righteousness, *(Acts 2:41)* and within a comparatively few days, thousands more. *(Acts 4:4)* The new species of Human Being, now known as the New Creation, is growing and increasing exponentially as the Good News is being preached unto the heirs of redemption, and the Lord is adding to the church daily, such as should be saved. *(Acts 2:47)*

The Book of Acts gives unto us the specific details of the early years of the church of the Lord Jesus Christ, and the past two Millennia have provided a historical record concerning what has occurred with this new species of humanity, known as the New Creation.

Sadly, the stark reality, within these last days in which we live, of what God has done concerning this New Creation Project, has been, for the most part, swallowed up by tradition and religion, and genuine spiritual truth is wanting. But that does not change the established reality of what was truly accomplished by the New Creation Jesus of Nazareth.

The future is bright and full of promise, and the clock is ticking away the remaining few minutes of opportunity that God has afforded unto all men.

FIFTEEN

The Super Natural Promise Fulfillment of the 21st Century: The Rapture

The early years of the Church of the Lord Jesus Christ were punctuated with power manifestation from on high. That punctuation period was directly followed by a he, that knew he, that knew him ministration; which was followed by religious-persecution-purging, and misused power administration. This period was followed by the Dark Ages of the hiding of the word of God off in monasteries; which was directly followed by the revelation of the just shall live by faith, and additionally followed by the early stages of the emanating forth of light once again. That period then, was followed by a Pentecostal explosion at the turn of the 20th century; which was followed by a healing revolution; which was followed by a charismatic emphasis; followed by a faith movement; which has subsequently brought us to the day of apostasy and departure from the word of truth.

In the eyes of some, these days are the current days of the authority of the believer. And for those who would press into the things of real eternal value, without allowing themselves to be deterred, the reality of that might be manifest. However, even as the Spirit of the Living God is being poured out upon all flesh throughout the globe, doubt, unbelief, carnality, and apostasy is the rule of the day, and not the exception, at least within the Western Hemisphere. *(II Thessalonians 2:3)* Immorality is running rampant; the traditions of men are chokingly overwhelming, and spiritual ignorance of Biblical truth, is at an all-time high.

Politically, here in the West, we are teetering on the edge of the precipice of destruction. The signs of *last days* realities are everywhere from the weather to military and social revolutions. However, within the midst of it all, there is an unchanging promise of a deliverance-from-wrath event that is soon to take place.

When the Apostle Paul wrote to the believers in the city of Corinth, he stated that he had received information concerning a spiritual event that heretofore was unknown, and was a mystery. *(I Corinthians 15:51-53)* He did not convey directly what the expected time-line might be as to when this mystery was to occur; but he had an expectation that it was going to happen within his own life time. Hindsight tells us that his expectation was ultimately something that did not come to pass.

Because of the extreme probability of this event being fulfilled within this 21st Century, discussion has ensued within circles of Christianity during preceding decades, and that discussion has even bled over into the secular arena, and precautions have been taken to make sure that the instantaneous disappearance and removal of tens of thousands of people, does not put those who remain here on this earth in jeopardy. Certain airlines have even adopted a policy that they will not put a born-again pilot and a born-again co-pilot in the same airplane, at the same time.

The event itself should gender excitement and anticipation within all true believers, considering all that is scheduled to take place in connection with the event fulfillment.

* First, the Rapture is a promised removal-from-wrath event for those who believe in it, and are looking for his return. *(I Thessalonians 5:9; Titus 2:13; Hebrews 9:28)* Prophetical fulfillment concerning the Nation of Israel is due to come to pass in short order, and a bulk of that fulfillment is the wrath of God being poured out upon this Earth. *(Revelation 16:1)* Genuine, hot, New Creation believers, are not slated to experience or endure that appointed wrath. *(I Thessalonians 5:9)*

* Secondly, the Rapture is not a haphazard occurrence as is put forth by the bulk of Christianity. *(Matthew 24:36)* It is a planned, scheduled event *(Amos 3:7)* due to be fulfilled precisely in line with the fifth of the declared Feasts of the Lord, that we find within the Book

of Leviticus. *(Leviticus 23:1; 24)* The Rapture has not been designed by God to be a *Surprise!* from the Lord, but rather, knowledge of the surety of the event should bring comfort. *(I Thessalonians 4:18)*

* Thirdly, the spirit/soul portions of the saints which slept *(I Thessalonians 4:13-15)* are to be carried by holy angels, from the Father's house in heaven, back here to the Earth, in order that they might receive, and be united with, their glorified Spiritual bodies *(I Corinthians 15:37-38; 42-44; I Thessalonians 4:16)* (i.e., these persons have experienced physical death, and are currently in a spirit/soul condition, and currently abide within the presence of the Lord) they are due to inherit a superior, Spiritual body, which will actually experience a granted release from many natural laws. *(I Corinthians 15:44)*

* Fourthly, genuine, hot, *(Revelation 3:16)* born-again, New Creations, that are still alive and well on planet Earth at the time of this event shall all be changed in a moment, *(I Corinthians 15:52)* and caught-up into the atmosphere of this globe. Physical corruption and mortality shall vanish in a flash, and incorruption and immortality shall take their place. *(I Corinthians 15:53)* A superior, glorified, Spiritual body awaits every born-again child of the Most High God. A reuniting of friends and family shall occur, *(I Thessalonians 4:17)* and we shall fly back with Jesus to the Father's house while tribulation, wrath, and destruction run its course on the planet surface. *(Matthew 24:21)*

* Fifthly, in this **author's opinion**, if you leave this Earth with one arm, you will arrive in heaven with one arm. If you leave this Earth overweight, you will arrive in heaven overweight. If you leave this Earth with scars and tattoos, you will arrive in heaven with scars and tattoos. There is no Scriptural basis for *presto change-o*, even when a Terrestrial body is replaced with a Spiritual body. There is a Scriptural precedent for spiritual authority over all of the handiwork of God's hands. *(Hebrews 2:8)* And there is a Scriptural foundation for speaking things that be not, as though they were, *(Romans 4:17)* and for there being nothing impossible. *(Matthew 17:20)* The problem has occurred is that we really do not believe, and we do not exercise and release faith; we only talk about it (however, the dead-in-Christ do not have this problem,

because their whole armless, tattooed, overweight body has disintegrated through decomposition, and they will receive a completely new, fully whole and functional Spiritual body, right away). So, when the Rapture event does occur, and we return to heaven, we shall be able to begin believing and releasing faith, and start speaking those things which be not, as though they were, right away . . . and in a relatively short period of time, the arm will be creatively replaced, the weight issue will become a moot point, and the scars and tattoos will fade and disappear. On the job training has now begun with those and other issues, and shall continue for the next 1,000 years, until the conforming to the image of Christ Jesus process is fully complete. *(Romans 8:29)*

There will be no more denominational Baptist, Methodist, Pentecostal, or any other religious schism, at the time of the Rapture. And any issue that would continue to gender division between members of the one Body of Christ will dissipate, and only children of a loving Father in heaven will remain.

When this event occurs, the grace of God, which came with the resurrection and appearance of the New Creation Jesus of Nazareth *(John 1:17)* will be withdrawn and removed from the Earth with the departure of the Rapture-candidate children of the Most High God. The whole of the Age of Grace that this world currently enjoys will then become a thing of the past. In Israel, the Law of Moses will once again be the order of the day, and the last vestiges of the wrath of God will follow shortly thereafter. *(Revelation 16:1)* The remainder of the Gentile world will find themselves in a *lawless* condition, and the misery that will ensue because of that will be beyond description. *(Matthew 24:21)*

The New Creation Project will be completely removed from the cosmic-stove focus, and ensconced in heaven, and the Nation of Israel on this Earth will once again be moved from the *back-burner* position on that stove, to the front.

SIXTEEN

The Jewish Nation of Israel Comes Back to the *Front-Burner* of the Stove, and Seven Years of Prophecy are Finally Fulfilled

One of the difficulties that we have in modern day Christianity, is the mixing-up of God's dealings with His Abrahamic Covenant, Chosen People, constituency of the Nation of Israel, persons. There is, in reality, an (A) first-part dealing to the Abrahamic Covenant, and in addition, there is a (B) second-part dealing as well.

The (A) first-part dealings are initiated and started with the actual covenant being cut and established within Genesis Chapter 15, and those dealings will officially end with the poured out wrath of God . . . death of the majority of the Jewish people remaining on the surface of this planet . . . dealing definitively with the Antichrist and the False Prophet . . . and completion of the Great Tribulation Period events, by the Second Coming of Jesus Christ of Nazareth to the Earth. *(Daniel 9:24; 27)*

There is an approximate 2,000 year spiritual-intermission within the cumulative (A) and (B) dealings, called "The Church Age," that occurs between the death of the Jewish Lord Jesus Christ of Nazareth and the removal-from-wrath mystery event known of as "The Rapture of the Church."

The (B) second-part dealings will initiate and start with the Nation of Israel "looking on him whom they have pierced," and receiving him as their king. *(Zechariah 12:10; Revelation 1:7)* And, by the way, there is no ending in sight to the (B) second-part dealings of the Abrahamic Blood Covenant. It continues to be in effect, on and on into the forever and ever.

During the spiritual-intermission, between all of the (A) first-part dealings of the Abrahamic Blood Covenant, and the (B) second-part dealings of the Abrahamic Blood Covenant, there is the insertion of the "New Creation, Body-of-Christ Project," and the Christian Blood Covenant, which is the Second Blood Covenant found named within the Scriptures. *(Hebrews 10:9)*

The Abrahamic Blood Covenant, whether it is the part (A) or the part (B), pertains only to the natural people of the Nation of Israel. Natural Gentiles are not ever included within covenantal activities. *(Unless they should convert to Judaism, in which case, they are not Gentiles any more) (Ephesians 2:12)* And all Supernatural New Creation individuals, called Christians, are not included within the Abrahamic Blood Covenant, because they have their own Christian Blood Covenant that they belong to, which is a better covenant, built upon better promises. *(Hebrews 8:6)* And, even though they are not part of the actual Abrahamic Blood Covenant, they will be operating within assigned positions of judgment *(I Corinthians 6:2-3)* and authority, within the covenant Nation of Israel, ruling and reigning with the New Creation Christ Jesus, during the last 1,000 years of this Probationary Period of Mankind.

The purpose of moving the Nation of Israel to the *back-burner* of the stove, was because they rejected the prophetical Promised One, murdered him, and removed him from the scene, and from any viability of covenant operations within the scenario of God's dealings with His people here on this Earth.

The purpose of moving the Nation of Israel back to the *front-burner* of the stove, is because the New Creation Body-of-Christ Project (of which the New Creation Jesus of Nazareth is the key individual) has been mostly completed, and summarily removed from the Earth. *(I Corinthians 15:51-53; I Thessalonians 4:16-17; Titus 2:13; Revelation 4:1)* And there is yet a seven-year prophetical *time-slice* that remains to be literally fulfilled concerning the part (A) dealings of the Abrahamic Covenant. *(Daniel 9:24; 27; Matthew 24:21)* At its origin and outset, Israel is in the precedent position, and there is no *Church* even in existence . . . Upon the resurrection of the New Creation Jesus of Nazareth, Israel is suspended, and the newly founded *Church* takes the precedent position. At a prophetical point in time, the *Church* is removed from the scene, and Israel is restored to the original precedent position once again; and that is how it works!

With the removal of the *Church* from the planet, there is no more operational-grace active on the Earth. *(The Dispensation of Grace will have concluded, and the Dispensation of Law is due to return to active operation, within the Nation of Israel.)*

The major world-class nation of the United States of America is shortly going to be removed from the scene, whether by economic-implosion, decadence, or revolution. The other large stabilizing nations of the world will follow suit, and the planet will plunge into a chaotic and disruptive condition; and, of course, it will all be the fault of the Nation of Israel. *(Tongue in cheek)* They are always the bad guys, are they not?

The Biblically declared, charismatic, Antichrist (who is right now, alive and well somewhere on planet Earth) will bubble-up to the surface, and feign benevolence and support for the hated, beleaguered, and despised Nation of Israel. The famous Peace Accord, between the Antichrist and the Nation of Israel, will be signed, *(Daniel 9:27)* and the next three and one-half years will unfold with a cacophony of events and happenings taking place that are both spiritual and natural in their nature. *(Book of Revelation)*

At the mid-point of the Tribulation Period, which is exactly 1,260 days from the signing of the Peace Accord: 144,000 zealous, Jewish, New Creations will be raptured from off of the face of the Earth *(Revelation 14:1)* . . . the prophets Enoch and Elijah will return to the Earth, after having been gone for 5,000 years and 3,500 years respectfully *(Revelation 11:3-4)* . . . Antichrist will step forward to show his true colors, and commit the ultimate abomination by declaring himself to be God. *(Matthew 24:15)* And the Great Tribulation and increased slaughter will commence, primarily against the Jewish people. *(Book of Revelation)*

During the last half of the Tribulation Period, which is exactly 1,260 days long, most of the Jewish people on planet Earth will perish.

Devastating natural and meteorological anomalies will be occurring all over the globe. Enoch and Elijah will be giving the Antichrist fits as they promote righteousness and repentance. And if the days of this devastation are not cut short, there will not be one surviving member amongst Mankind. All persons on the face of the planet will be destroyed. *(Matthew 24:21)*

Happily, the grim picture that the Tribulation Period paints does not last long. With the last vestiges of God's wrath, poured out upon sin and rebellion; *(Revelation 16:1)* and with the resurrection and ascension of the murdered Enoch and Elijah at the end of the Great Tribulation, *(Revelation 11:7-12)* the New Creation Jesus of Nazareth will split the Eastern sky, to fulfill his Second Coming, rescue of His Chosen People, promise. *(Revelation 19:11-16)*

SEVENTEEN

Antichrist is Dead, The Devil is Bound, and a 1,000 Year Reign Begins

The deluded Antichrist, because he has had an assist from the *signs and wonders* false prophet, *(Revelation 13:11-14)* believes that he will be able to defeat the returning New Creation Jesus of Nazareth. Such is not the case. Upon the Second Coming of Christ, the Antichrist and the False Prophet are promptly arrested, and thrown alive into the Lake of Fire. They are the first two inhabitants within that particular compartment of Hell. *(Revelation 19:20)* Their bodies shall be burned-up upon their entrance, and they shall be screaming in excruciating pain, at the top of their lungs, for the next 1,000 years before they are joined by Satan himself.

Michael, the chief angelic prince of the Nation of Israel, *(Daniel 10:13)* is then called upon to bind his fallen-angelic associate, Satan. *(Revelation 20:1-3)* Within the solitary confinement of the Bottomless Pit, and having ample opportunity to *think-it-over* throughout the next 1,000 years, *(Revelation 20:3)* you might think that Satan would get an epiphany concerning the futility of coming against the Living God or His Christ. Such is not the case.

The purpose behind the 1,000 year, Millennial Reign of the Lord Jesus Christ is multi-faceted.

* For the natural, Jewish, Nation of Israel, it will be the initial realization of the completed promise of blessings from the God who built them, and then covenantally wed them. *(Ezekiel 16:3-8; Hosea 2:19-20)* Continued fulfillment of those covenant blessings and promises shall extend into the eternal everlasting ahead.

* For the New Creation Lord Jesus, it will be the time for a governmental establishment of a manifested kingdom, *(Isaiah 9:6; Colossians*

1:13) and a rod-of-iron ruler ship, during the wrap-up of a probational work. *(Romans 9:28; Revelation 2:27 & 19:15)*

* For the New Creation brothers and sisters, of the New Creation Jesus of Nazareth, it will be a time of instruction, training, and exercising of the faith that we are supposed to be living by, right now. *(Habakkuk 2:4; Romans 1:17; Galatians 3:11; Hebrews 10:38)* In the millennium, talk will turn into action, and co-reigning authority and judgmental actions will be part-and-parcel of the process. *(I Corinthians 6:2-3; Revelation 20:4)*

* For the Earth, it will be a time of cleansing from all of the effects of Sin. *(II Peter 3:10-12)* The three Basic Creation Elements of Air, Water, and Soil will be augmented into an active operation, without the devastating effects of pollution of any kind.

* For the Gentile nations, it will be a time of life without hassles. Hatred, selfishness, theft, and deception will not be the order of the day. The Law of Sin will still be in existence, but its active operation within Earth's society is no more. Business endeavors, pro-creation, recreation and development, will be in their full-swing operational modes. Some Gentiles will choose to join the Nation of Israel and convert to Judaism because of a covenant advantage, but the majority of them will not. They will enjoy all of the benefits of life, but they will be on the lowest rung of the ladder, to be sure, as far as Human Beings go. Through continued obedience to the simple rules that apply, they shall be able to live forever, and enjoy the natural creation of God.

EIGHTEEN

Devil is Gone, Sinners are Judged, and the Heavenly City of New Jerusalem Descends From Heaven

One thousand years will pass, as fast as one thousand years usually passes. Should there be any death incidents that occur within that time frame, anywhere on the Earth, it will be an extremely nominal occurrence, at best.

All of the aspects of natural life are in a full-swing operation: Sleeping, Eating, Personal Hygiene, Sexual Activity, Mandatory Labor, and Leisure Time. Acknowledgment and worship of the One True God is ongoing, and men are living their lives to the fullest.

As the end of the millennia draws near, a flurry of activity, once again, begins to occur:

* Satan, who has been bound and incarcerated for the last 1,000 years of time, is loosed from his imprisonment. *(Revelation 20:7)*

* Upon his release, he immediately begins to travel around the world, looking for the malcontents who greatly desire to overthrow the iron-rule that they have been living under for the last ten centuries. *(Revelation 20:8)*

* The dissidents are ripe for the picking, and Satan begins to accumulate a sizable number of rebels. His purpose is, of course, that of insurrection. One thousand years of solitary incarceration have taught him nothing. His thinking is such, that he is persuaded, that if he can accumulate a sufficient number of soldiers, he can assault and defeat the reigning king of Jerusalem. *(Revelation 20:9)*

* The city of the New Jerusalem, has been traveling at the speed of light, in its relocation process, from the planet named Heaven, unto a close-proximity to the planet named Earth. It is due to arrive at its destination very shortly. *(Revelation 21:2)*

* Having gathered his forces, Satan attempts a surrounding of, and assaulting of, the city of earthly Jerusalem. However, before he can even come close, fire from a loving heavenly Father, rains down upon the hordes of rebels, and they are burned-up. *(Revelation 20:9)*

* The destruction-by-fire of the rebellious multitude, results in Satan being cast directly into the Lake of Fire compartment of the Nether World, and the spirit/soul complement of the crispy-critter constituency being deposited into the Hades compartment of the Nether World to await finalities. *(Revelation 20:10)*

* With the final spurt of rebellion being nipped in the bud, the time has finally come that all rebels have dreaded since the days of Adam . . . JUDGMENT DAY!

* In order to qualify as a participant in this exciting activity, a Human Being must have been physically born onto planet Earth, and in addition, at least once, physically died. *(Hebrews 9:27)*

* The actual judgment takes place in the presence of God, which means that the designated location for this event to occur, is in heaven, and not on the planet, Earth. *(Revelation 20:11-12)*

* The Judge who will be sitting on the judgment seat, and rendering righteous justice, is the New Creation Jesus of Nazareth. *(John 5:22)*

* The Prosecutor *(which may or may not be the Holy Spirit of God)* is not mentioned and may indeed also be the Lord Jesus Christ. But, whatever the case may be, the recorded charges against each spiritual criminal *(Revelation 20:12)* . . . which will include every single unrighteous thought, word, and deed, from the time of their natural birth until they stand before Judge Jesus, will be read aloud, and the question posed: How do you plead, Guilty, or Not Guilty? The evidence against each individual will be so overwhelming that a response of "Not Guilty" will not even be possible. Hence, each spiritual criminal will ultimately utter their own sentence of condemnation and separation from God, and that sentence shall be carried out by the holy angels, almost immediately. God will effectively send no one into Hell because that awful action would conflict with His nature of Love. *(II Peter 3:9)*

* A casting forth into the Lake of Fire will cause the recently resurrected natural bodies of the damned, to be burned-up, and experience a physical Second Death. *(John 5:28-29; Revelation 21:8)*

* While required judgmental actions are occurring in heaven, life's natural activities and business-as-usual transactions are taking place on the Earth. It is quite possible that the natural Jew and Gentile inhabitants of the Earth will not even be aware of what is transpiring, judgment wise, right above their heads.

* As unpleasant and gut-retching as the Judgment Day realities might have been, it was indeed necessary to preserve the harmony of all of God's creation for the unending eons that lay stretched out into the horizon-less future ahead.

* With the conclusion of the last probational event, the holy city of the New Jerusalem will appear on the spiritual radar screen. *(Revelation 21:2)*

NINETEEN

Eternity Begins — What to Expect

All of the foreknowledge activities of both the Angelic Probational Period, and the Probation of Mankind, are now complete. So, what is next?

Well, the New Creation Jesus of Nazareth has been reigning as king over the Jewish Nation of Israel, for the last one thousand years, to get the ball rolling for all of eternity. The kingdom is the manifested and declared kingdom of God's dear Son *(Colossians 1:13)* that we know of as the Kingdom of Heaven *(Matthew 4:17)* that has been in full swing on the Earth for the last millennia. It is a Jewish kingdom that has been established for the Jewish people, because of covenant promises. *(There is no Gentile kingdom because there is no Gentile covenant with the living God, that is in place.)* The promise that was made, was made to a Jewish man (First, to King David and then, to King Jesus) *(II Samuel 7:12-29)* that he would be ruling over a Jewish kingdom. The probation for Mankind, now being over, the New Creation Jesus of Nazareth's assignment within the capacity of that Kingdom of Heaven, is now fulfilled, and has come to a conclusion. New Creation Jesus of Nazareth will now pass the reigning scepter over to the resurrected, New Creation King David, to whom the throne was originally promised by God the Father. *(II Samuel 7:12-29)* The New Creation King David's eternal assignment is going to be one of governance. He is the one that will be reigning over the Kingdom of Heaven, here on this Earth, forever. *(Ezekiel 37:20-28)*

The holy city that God the Father built long ago, which has foundations, *(Hebrews 11:10)* has now arrived above the atmosphere of this planet Earth. *(Revelation 21:2)* It is now time for the New Creation, children of the Most High God, *(Ephesians 1:5; I John 3:1)* to move into their new mansions, and permanently establish their residence. The New Creation Jesus of Nazareth will also pack his suitcase, and permanently move into the holy city of the New Jerusalem. Whether he will move into his own personal mansion, or take up residence, and live, within the Temple that is within the city, *(Hebrews 8:2)* is not yet clear. He will then have his name changed, *(Revelation 3:12)* and his eternal focus will shift from the Nation of Israel, to the expanse of the remainder of the entire created universe.

The only permanent residents of the holy city the New Jerusalem, will be God the Father, God the Father's Only Begotten Son (he whom we know of today, as New Creation Jesus of Nazareth), all of God the Father's adopted children, *(Ephesians 1:5)* and the Holy Spirit of God, who dwells within all of the children of God the Father, as well as being able to operate in an independent manner Himself. It is in reality, a genuine family affair. It is the City of the Immortals. *(I Corinthians 15:53)* The city was expressly built to become established as the very household of the Creator of all things.

The basic issues of life, that we are now acquainted with, on a 24 hour time-cycle basis, are: mandatory eating, mandatory sleeping, mandatory personal hygiene, optional sexual activity, mandatory labor, optional leisure time, and established focused worship of the Most High God. And, as for the natural Jew and natural Gentile constituency, whether living on this Earth, or on any other planet, those 24 hour time-cycle issues will still remain the same, for evermore.

The basic issues of life, that the New Creation, immortal, children of the Most High God, shall become acquainted with, on a 24 hour time-cycle basis, might be: optional eating (because of immortality), elimination of sleeping (because of immortality), optional personal hygiene (for fastidiousness, and not for waste disposal—there is no waste disposal because of immortality), optional sexual activity (an issue that is so sensitive that it is conversationally, actively avoided by Christianity), mandatory labor (because there will be things to do, places to go, and people to see, forever), optional leisure time (because to every thing there is a season, and a time to every purpose under the heaven), *(Ecclesiastes 3:1)* and established focused worship of the Most High God. And any of the changes that we will experience concerning those issues, indeed will be because of the effect that immortality will have had upon our personage. It is in concept, the reality of having absolutely no connection with the condition of death, in any of its manifestations or conditions.

The holy city of the New Jerusalem, will become established as the headquarters of Universal Administration, Governance, and Maintenance. At given points in time, children of the Most High God, shall report to the executive office in order to receive their *task* assignments for their mandatory labor. At this point in time, being now conformed to the image of Christ, *(Romans 8:29)* we will actually be exercising, and operating in the *mountain moving* faith that Jesus told us about in the gospels. *(Mark 11:22-24)* So, we may be given an assignment to travel to a specified location within a distant star system, for the purpose of preparing a planet for habitation by a natural Jewish or Gentile constituency.—No spaceship is needed. No spacesuit is needed. No special tools are needed, other than the words of creative power that utter forth from our lips. We will be speaking things that be not, as though they were, *(Romans 4:17)* and watching as the elements of creation move as they are directed, and enjoying the results as creative vision occurs.

For the natural Jewish and Gentile constituency, they shall continue to reproduce and multiply upon the face of this Earth until more space is needed, and then, colonization for Mankind begins to commence out into the various regions of this universe. The planet Earth will become the universal headquarters for the Colonization of Mankind. When this occurs, there will be a need for a spaceship, and for spacesuits. There will be a need for a Captain Kirk to pilot the spaceship. These individuals are still natural and shall never become immortal. These individuals require an atmosphere to breathe. They are required to sleep, to rejuvenate their strength. They are required to eat to refuel their natural terrestrial bodies. They are required to use the restroom for waste removal, because, in simplicity, the natural physical body is just a tube; what goes in, will eventually come out. They will continually need both the fruit and leaves from the Tree of Life to eternally sustain them, because they are not immortal, they are yet natural and technically mortal.

For those who somehow believe that heaven is one big white room, with individual clouds for the people who are there to sit upon; and that a little golden harp is standard government issue, so that we can play our harps in worship unto God. . . . Or, for those who somehow believe that the whole purpose for heaven is so that we are able to have one continuous, glorious, 24/7 worship service because God is deserving of all of the praise. . . . Or, for those who somehow believe that heaven consists of having an ideal tee-time of 9:00 a.m., day after day, or that heaven is there to provide a steady stream of Super Bowl games to watch, or a relaxing, blissful time of planting flowers within the mansion garden, or of visiting with grandma or grandpa for the first ten years, or of going fishing, or of the taking care of the domesticated cats, dogs, horses or cows, this author prays that they are not going to be too disappointed when they get there, and find out that, that is not really the case. This is not how it works at all. God is an adult. And God expects to be dealing with other adults, within the extensive plans that He has for us. It is wise to consult the Word of God for insight into all of those things, particularly eternity, which continues a whole lot longer that the short life-span that we are consigned to, this side of everlasting.

TWENTY

Visions of the Future

Over the process of time, as this author has focused on subjects of eternal value, the Lord has graciously granted unto him two specific visions of potential future *happenings*.

These visions do not violate Scriptural parameters, but rather present a projected scenario of what believers in the Lord Jesus Christ may experience within the millennia that lie out ahead. Take a moment if you will, step into the shoes, and savor what may become a very real experience for you, much sooner than you think.

Picture, if you will, a small rural town in the Midwest that is not unlike 'Mayberry RFD.' It is a bright mid morning, and a summer sleepiness hangs in the air. A young mother, on an errand, is walking up the quiet street with her young son in tow. As they are walking, the young son suddenly freezes in his tracks, his eyes fixed on two figures walking toward them on the same side of the street. The mother is pulled up short and is unable to budge the young boy who is mesmerized by the sight. The two figures, walking slowly, and exuding a radiance of intense light, reach and then pass the mother and son, smiling graciously and nodding as they do. The young boy's eyes are riveted on their every step.

When the two figures are safely out of voice range, the young son tugs feverishly at his mother's skirt, and anxiously asks, "Mother, mother, who are those people?"

With a confident understanding, the mother smiles sweetly, looks down into her young son's eyes, and replies, "They, my son, are the children of the Most High God."

The future that our God has planned for those who love Him, far surpasses anything that this world has to offer.

The time has come to begin the expansion. Probation was necessarily both painful and extremely sad, but now it is concluded and we can move on. 'Supernatural' sons and daughters of a loving Father have enjoyed over 1,000 years of personal training in the exercising of their faith, and in their on-the-job ruler ship maneuvers during the 'conforming' process, in becoming carbon copies of the Only Begotten. They have shared in judgment responsibilities and are now qualified to advance in their training. It is time for their honed skills to be demonstrated 'in the field.'

A call goes forth for a chosen child to report to the executive office for assignment. A Divine memo gives explicit and detailed instruction concerning planetary preparation for the intended new colony. Travel arrangements are diligently made and departure takes place toward the selected location.

Gliding through the star clusters and perspective worlds of the future is intoxicating beyond description. Colors exceeding brilliant, indescribable formations, and a virtual weaving of gas and light, that pulsates hypnotically, is seemingly everywhere.

Arriving at the intended destination, a quick survey provides substantiation of what needs to be done. From a given locale on the surface of the planet, the son of glory utters decrees of adjustment to the elements of the atmosphere. There is no hesitation as to the compliance of the directive. Various gases begin to increase and then decrease, and ultimately reach a desired balance. Schematic wind circuitry, clouds for moisture administration, and the 'day' time and 'night' time necessities are brought unto a point of harmony.

The existing land formations are much too harsh to utilize, and certain portions of the mountains need to be relocated to provide for optimum benefit. Commands are given and the elements respond. Water is scarce, so established Basic Creation Elements need to be brought onto the scene and utilized to establish all that is needed for a pristine habitation.

A final global survey at the tasks end confirms that the new locale is now acceptable, and the ship of populous can arrive at their scheduled discretion. Colonization should be able to commence without any further difficulty.

A leisurely trip of return is quite relaxing, and upon reaching home the eternal mansion is indeed a welcomed sight. Aah, worship is scheduled for the morning, and hearts and hands shall be raised in exaltation of the Regent of Glory. Peace beyond understanding, love, harmony, joy, and fulfillment in every aspect of life once again permeates every fiber of his being. With assignment completed, his heart and his home have been united once again.

This work is short, and the subject is enormous, but we pray that some of the information contained within these pages has provided insight, and has been a blessing. God is not willing that any should perish, *(II Peter 3:9)* so share this work with others so that they too may be able to take advantage of the free gift of salvation, through a personal relationship with the New Creation Lord of Glory. May God's blessing be upon you as you do.

Keep your eyes looking upward . . . Maranatha! the Lord cometh.

Part Two

Angelic Social Order

Is there the possibility of an **Angelic Social Order?**
What do the holy scriptures reveal concerning an active Angelic Society?

Introduction

Who ever heard of an Angelic Society? Just the idea that angels would be involved in the same kind of, or similar, activities that we find Humans involved in, is almost ludicrous to most people, is it not?

Angels just fly around and do what God tells them to do, don't they? They simply stand before His throne and cry Holy, Holy, Holy continually, don't they? They are only ministering spirits sent forth to minister for those who shall be the heirs of salvation, aren't they? *(Hebrews 1:14)*

This subject is unique, to say the least. Usually, the focus of Christianity is . . . get people saved . . . get people saved . . . get people saved — build the Church . . . build the Church . . . build the Church. And please do not misunderstand, this author wholeheartedly believes in getting people saved, and in building the Church. But, he also believes in growing people up, spiritually. God is the One who says that His people are destroyed for lack of knowledge. *(Hosea 4:6)* And this 21st Century generation is grossly undereducated in their knowledge of what the Scriptures teach.

This subject is not going to send people to Hell if they do not know about this information, or assure people of their reward in heaven if they do. But it might make people a little more knowledgeable concerning things operating within an invisible realm.

So, come with us for a short tour through some Scriptural notations that are put forth concerning angels, and at least consider what is additionally presented. You may be blessed as you do.

ONE

What Might Be the Possibility?

The New Webster's Dictionary defines a Society as, *"the state of living in organized groups; any number of people (individuals) associated together geographically, racially, or otherwise with collective interests; a civil or business association organized under the law; that part of a community considered to be the elite by birth, wealth, or culture, etc."*

Within this world in which we live, as we focus on the happenings that are going on all around us, we are able to drink-in, and consider, the myriad of elements that potentially make up any given *Society*.

There certainly are cultural differences, geographical differences, economical differences, even demographic differences; but in this world, people are still people, wherever one goes. So whether we are white, or black, or red, or yellow; whether we are tall or short, or thin, or fat; whether we are rich, or poor, or smart, or ignorant . . . people are still people, they will still do what people do, and be involved in all of the things that people are involved with.

When we go to the Scriptures, and study, and consider *The World That Then Was,* (II Peter 3:6) we will find information that clearly indicates that a complete and active *Society* existed on this planet prior to the creation of Adam and Eve. *(Psalm 104:5-7; Isaiah 14:13-14; Jeremiah 4:23-26; Ezekiel 28:15-19)* Those individuals that made up that constituency, it would seem, were intelligent, and moral, and free-thinking. It is only logical to assume, that they had things to do, and places to go, and other individuals to see. But, they still interacted with one another, accomplished certain tasks, and were involved with all of the other various elements that we understand would be operating within any given *Society*.

So, when we take the time to consider the intelligent, moral, and free willed individuals that we know of, and refer to, as angels . . . why might it be any different? Simply because we are not aware of, or fail to understand, what may be involved, does not negate the possibility, or cancel the reality of its existence.

Within this universe, there exists the Omnipotent Creator Himself, and the three *Creation Categories* of intelligent beings that He has brought forth for His own good pleasure. *(Ephesians 1:5 & 9; Philippians 2:13)* Those created creatures, for the three *Creation Categories*, in the order of their positions and importance, are from the bottom to the top: *Other Creatures, Angelic Hosts and Mankind.*

The obedient *Other Creatures* are currently dwelling within known societal parameters, wherever they may be located within this universe. *(Colossians 1:16)* And for those *Other Creatures* that originated from this planet *(Romans 8:39)* who have rebelled against God, and whom we know of today as *Demons*: they have once lived within societal parameters in the past, prior to their rebellion.

Mankind is also currently dwelling within known societal parameters, and will continue to do so, even into the everlasting that is stretched out beyond any horizon; whether on this planet Earth, or as colonization takes place on other planets within this universe.

Are *Angels* actually going to be established by a non-respecter of persons, God of grace, within different operating parameters? Are their assignments such, that they are stationed 24/7 within duty responsibilities? Have they no *free-time*, with which to pursue other endeavors? Are there really no other endeavors to pursue? Is there of a certainty no interaction between glorious creations of love, when the other two levels of created creatures that they have regular dealings with, do interact within their *Societies*? We just might want to take a few minutes, and a second look, to rethink that which we *know* so well.

The Holy Scriptures are given unto us by God, to be our definitive source of information concerning these kinds of questions. May we take some time and look at what they reveal to us, concerning the whole contingency of Angelic Hosts.

TWO

What Do the Scriptures Say About Angelic Individuals?

What kind of beings are Angels anyway?

As the Omnipotent Creator is a spirit being Himself, *(John 4:24)* He has brought forth all three *Creation Categories* of moral creatures that He has created, as spirit beings, as well.

All Angels are spirit beings. *(Hebrews 1:14)* As such, the spirit portion of their being is the primary invisible-force of their personage, and has been designed by God to receive instruction, and carry designated responsibility for their actions.

All Angels have been gifted with a soul containing Intelligence, Emotions, and a Free will. As such, the soul portion of their being is the secondary invisible-force of their personage, that has been designed by God to augment and assist facilitation between their spirit and their Celestial Body.

And all Angels have bodies, or tabernacles, in which dwell both the spirit and the soul portions of their beings. Of the three different types of bodies that exist, *(I Corinthians 15:40; 44)* the Angels have been gifted with the Celestial Body. These celestial tabernacles are possibly *constructed* or manufactured, using the Basic Creation Element of Air, that is combined with a Divinely infused, prophetical declaration from God. *(Psalm 33:6; 148:1-5)* God did not just magically say, "Let there be . . . and . . . POOF! . . . there was". There are Creation Laws that are involved. Celestial Bodies, it would seem according to Scriptural records, are not subject to the real condition of *physical death*, suspended operation, or eventual decay, as we know occurs with Terrestrial Bodies. Even with certain angelic beings, still operating within a sinful condition, these Celestial Bodies continue to function according to

Divine design, *(Job 1:6-7; 2:1-2)* and must be restrained using real chains, *(II Peter 2:4; Jude 6; Revelation 20:1)* or a specific locale of incarceration. *(Matthew 25:41)* Angels are Eternal in their original design and construct, having the capacity to live forever with God, if obedience is maintained and the established *rules* are adhered to.

The angelic Celestial Bodies that they live in, are not designed for normal reproduction as we know it, and thus an increase of the angelic ranks, mainly because of the absence of female compliments. There is no Scriptural record, anywhere, of any female Angels. Even so, there are many Angels that are formatted, within a foreknowledge-sphere parameter, into a male/humanoid configuration, which is inclusive of operational plumbing. *(Genesis 6:2; 4; Jude 6-7)*

Although we have established, reliable records of Scripture, that reference *angels food* per se, as to what that food may consist of is unknown at this time. All created bodies are in need of some sort of nourishment, whether Terrestrial, Celestial, or Spiritual. These Celestial Bodies may differ markedly in their appearance, and they may function differently as well, in their operational assignments; however, they are nonetheless Celestial in design and construct, and are capable of functioning equally well, within both the spiritual and the natural realms, with precise effectiveness.

We have no established Scriptural record of any type of disruption, or separation, between the spirit and the soul compliments and the Celestial Body, of any disobedient, rebellious, fallen Angel. Sin and its entry-level consequence of spiritual death, is what normally causes any disruption, or separation, within the construct of various free-will, moral beings in the first place. And only those angelic beings that have rebelled against God, and disobeyed His loyalty requirements, and are willing subjects of the Law of Sin, experience the entry-level, spiritual death consequences of sin. But that spiritual death consequence does not seem to affect their Celestial Bodies in any manifested, perceivable manner. Whether, in the future, a Celestial Body, inhabited by a rebellious Angel, after judgment and sentence pronouncement,

(I Corinthians 6:3) is able to burn-up and be destroyed within the Lake of Fire, is a remains-to-be-seen reality.

All Angels have the power of flight, or the ability to ascend and descend at their own discretion, due to their Celestial Body capabilities. In a converse manner, any created moral creature: a Man, or an Angel, or an Other Creature, does not possess the innate ability to *fly*, absent from either their Celestial, Terrestrial, or Spiritual Body housing. In other words, disembodied spirit-beings, from any of the three Creation Categories, cannot *fly*.

And the flight capability of any Angel is not dependent upon whether or not they have wings. There are some Angels that have been designed with six wings, *(Isaiah 6:2)* and some Angels that have been designed with four wings, *(Ezekiel 10:21)* and some Angels that have been designed with only two wings, as we have become familiar with in most of the drawings and pictures that we have seen. However, there is also a constituency of angels that have no wings at all, *(Hebrews 13:2)* and are humanoid in their appearance; but the absence of wings does not mean that they cannot *fly*. Since all Angels, whether they are fallen or obedient, possess the power of flight, that *flight-quality* alone should explain to us that Angels and *Other Creatures* are coming forth from two completely separate *Creation Categories*.

Angels that have disobeyed and rebelled against God, would now be definitively known of, as Fallen Angels, and should not be referred to as Demons, as some Scripturally-uninformed men would attempt to do. These Fallen Angels would still have the use of their Celestial Bodies, even though they are in an actively sinful condition. They would also still have the power of flight, even though they are in a fallen, disobedient, state. They would still categorically be known of as Angels, even though they have fallen from the position of the grace that they were created in, and once held.

Previous *Other Creature* category individuals, now to be known by us as Demons, do not possess any bodies to work in at all; which is why they want to take up residence, and live, within the Terrestrial Bodies of Human men and women; or at the very least, be able to live within various members of the animal complement of this Social Order. *(Mark 5:8-14)*

Since demons cannot *fly*, of a necessity, they must catch the local bus, or ride in someone's car, or book a flight on an airliner, or hitch a ride on someone's bicycle, or at the very least, submit to walking. *(Matthew 12:43)* In short, very real creatures called demons are not Angels, fallen or otherwise, and various angelic creations, even though they have rebelled and sinfully disobeyed God, are not demons.

THREE

What is it That Angels Do?

#1. ***"So he drove out the man; and he placed at the east of the garden of Eden Cherubims, and a flaming sword which turned every way, to keep the way of the tree of life."*** *(Genesis 3:24)*

Chronologically speaking, this is the first appearance of Angels, within the Scriptural account. A cherub is, in fact, an angelic rank, held by a mature male angel, with designated responsibilities; and not some cute, plump, rosy-colored, baby Angel with tiny wings. It would seem that the cherubim operate as the guardians within the angelic societal-structure. Within this Scriptural notation above, they were placed outside of the Garden of Eden's eastern gate, after the imposed eviction of the residents, to prevent Adam and Eve from having an entrance back into the Garden, and unfettered access to the Tree of Life. This protective measure remained in place, until such a time as the Tree of Life was once again able to be transplanted from the Earth, back into the city of New Jerusalem from whence it originally came.

Within the Book of Exodus, cherubim are symbolically placed in a position of guardianship over the established Mercy Seat, within the Holy of Holies, in the wilderness tabernacle-of-the-congregation. *(Exodus 25:18-22)* Since Moses was admonished by God, to make the tabernacle on Earth, after the pattern that was shown unto him in the mount, of the actual tabernacle that is in heaven, *(Hebrews 8:5)* is it probable or even possible, that the genuine Mercy Seat within the true tabernacle in heaven is also guarded by responsible Angels?

#2. "That the sons of God saw the daughters of men that they were fair; and they took them wives of all which they chose." (Genesis 6:2)

"There were giants in the earth in those days; and also after that, when the sons of God came in unto the daughters of men, and they bare children to them, the same became mighty men which were of old, men of renown." (Genesis 6:4)

    These two verses are both understandably clear, and controversial, at the same time. For those individuals who are **"willingly ignorant of, that by the word of God, the heavens were of old, and the earth standing out of the water and in the water: whereby the world that then was, being overflowed with water, perished:"** (II Peter 3:5-6) these verses are quite controversial. But for those individuals who understand that there really was an active Social Order operating on planet Earth, before Adam and Eve were even created, these verses are understandable and knowledgably clear.

    May we understand first and foremost, that the *sons of God* that are being referred to here within these verses, are angelic beings that are *sons of God* by virtue of direct creation, and not because of any birthing process. And secondly, that these Angels are, sadly, fallen from grace and are the servants of Satan. *(Romans 6:16)* Satan is the despot who commanded these agents to lie to and deceive, and then cohabitate with Human women, so that half Fallen-Angelic and half authoritative-Human offspring-children could be born. The ultimate intent of that union was the defiling of the pure Adamic Human bloodline; so that the prophesied Redeemer of Genesis 3:15 would not ever be able to come forth.

    Before the flood of Noah, the most famous of these co-habitational, unredeemable-offspring products, would be a man of renown named Hercules. And after the cleansing and purifying action of the flood, even though it took a period of time for Satan to put the *"also after that"* into effect, the most renown of these off-spring products, would be the Philistine man named Goliath.

However, an important nuance to the abominable activity that these verses reveal, is the knowledge that certain humanoid-in-appearance Angels possess reproductive plumbing; inclusive of genitals, operational capacity thereof, and blood production seed-potential. So, when Angels leave their first estate, and keep not their own habitation, *(Jude 6)* is there somehow an alteration that occurs to their Celestial Bodies? If there is, we may not become aware of the details of exactly how that occurs, until after the Probational Period for Mankind is concluded.

#3. ***"And when the morning arose, then the angels hastened Lot, saying, Arise, take thy wife, and thy two daughters, which are here; lest thou be consumed in the iniquity of the city.***

And while he lingered, the men laid hold upon his hand, and upon the hand of his wife, and upon the hand of his two daughters; the Lord being merciful unto him: and they brought him forth, and set him without the city." *(Genesis 19:15-16)*

Here is the incident of the famed cities of Sodom and Gomorrah. And we can readily see that the Angels literally had to drag Lot and his family out of the city before the destruction and devastation came forth.

It would seem, from the numerous Scriptural accounts that we have, that Holy Angels have been granted a particular involvement within judgmental activities, during the Probational Period. This account of Sodom and Gomorrah is just one of them.

The Angels are not acting by reason of their own volition, or according to their own discretion. They are responding to the directives that God has issued, within a given situation.

People anguish and struggle, concerning the subject of judgment; Christian people in particular. And at least one of the reasons for that is because Christian people know: *God is Love (I John 4:8)* And they do not understand how a God of love can be involved in all of these heinous judgmental activities, where sometimes *innocent* people die.

The bottom line is found within the original laws that have been ordained and established, concerning all things that shall come into, and then be maintained and operate, in existence. Any given cause shall have a particular effect. What goes up, without any outside influence, must certainly come down. Whatsoever a man soweth, that shall he also reap. *(Galatians 6:7)* And the monkey-wrench that has been thrown into the cornucopia reservoir of creative laws, is the heinous Law of Sin. Because of the very nature of the Law of Sin, it automatically adversely interacts with various other *neutral* creative laws, and the morphed product that comes forth is a law that is destructive, particularly where judgment is concerned.

We are not looking at the personal character of either Angels or God, when we observe these judgmental situations, we are looking at the consequence of morphed laws. And judgment finds its whole basis for operation, and validity, within those morphed laws.

It is sadly true that Angels, whether holy or unholy, at various points in time, kill Human people. Not because they hate the people, (at least on the side of Holy Angels) but because of judgmental necessity. They are not displaying personal angst during the process, they are simply carrying out specific orders. And those orders find their issuance directives within the newly established morphed laws, whether we understand how that works or not.

Within the situation of the Sodom and Gomorrah judgment, Angels may not be specifically the ones who will rain down the fire and brimstone upon the city, but they certainly were involved, and do give the warning that is sent from God, and rescue those who are Biblically referred to as being righteous.

#4. "And when the angel stretched out his hand upon Jerusalem to destroy it, the Lord repented him of the evil, and said to the angel that destroyed the people, It is enough: stay now thine hand. And the angel of the Lord was by the threshing place of Araunah the Jebusite." *(II Samuel 24:16)*

This incident involves King David and his willful disobedience of numbering the children of Israel after both God and men had advised him not to. Sadly, the cost for this transgression was the forfeited lives of seventy thousand men, executed by angelic judgmental agents of God. And the inhabitants of the city of Jerusalem escaped the same slated fate—by God's mercy—and repentance of what newly established morphed laws would have ordinarily demanded.

#5. *"And he answered, Fear not: for they that be with us are more than they that be with them.*
And Elisha prayed, and said, Lord I pray thee, open his eyes, that he may see. And the Lord opened the eyes of the young man; and he saw: and, behold the mountain was full of horses and chariots of fire round about Elisha." *(II Kings 6:16-17)*

Within this Scriptural incident, it was during the night that a multitude of horses and chariots came from the king of Syria, to the Israeli city of Dothan, to surround Elisha the prophet of God. And when Elisha's servant became quite fearful because of the number of enemies that he saw, Elisha petitioned God to open the young man's eyes that he might see the angelic host of horses and chariots that God supplied, to surround and outnumber the imposing forces of the king.

Those horses and chariots continually dwell within the invisible realm of the spirit, and those chariots were actually being driven by holy angelic agents of the Lord.

#6. *"Then said Daniel unto the king, O king, live forever.*
My God hath sent his angel, and hath shut the lion's mouths, that they have not hurt me: forasmuch as before him innocency was found in me; and also before thee, O king, have I done no hurt." *(Daniel 6:21-22)*

In this particular situation, a Holy Angel of God was dispatched to provide physical protection for a covenant man that was in trouble; a man that was placed in harm's way and was desired to be eaten by hungry lions. The Angel fulfilled his commission, and the covenant man emerged from the situation unharmed.

#7. "Bless the Lord, ye his angels, that excel in strength, that do his commandments, hearkening unto the voice of his word." *(Psalm 103:30)*

There are three areas of insight that are afforded unto us concerning Angels, within this verse in the Book of Psalms. In their manufacturing design construct, Angels are much more powerful than regular men, and are able to defeat regular men in any potential physical-strength conflict; which is why the unredeemable offspring of Fallen Angels (Hercules and Goliath, just to name two) are renown, and looked upon as being *super-human*. Secondly, the mention of *commandments* within the verse, is not referring to the Ten Commandments, which were given by God to the Nation of Israel; but rather, to the divine directives that are uttered by God to Angels as task decrees. And additionally, since the word of God is forever settled in heaven, *(Psalm 119:89)* any and all decrees of divine direction will be solely based upon the written word of God that we are privileged to have and work with. God does not speak to the whole of His creation through His word, and then just utter any other statements that are not harmonious to what the Holy Scriptures plainly declare.

#8. "Yea, whiles I was speaking in prayer, even the man Gabriel, whom I had seen in the vision at the beginning, being caused to fly swiftly, touched me about the time of the evening oblation.
And he informed me, and talked with me, and said, O Daniel, I am now come forth to give thee skill and understanding.
At the beginning of thy supplications the commandment came forth, and I am come to shew thee; for thou art greatly beloved: therefore, understand the matter, and consider the vision." *(Daniel 9:21-23)*

Part of angelic responsibility includes bringing answers to prayer requests. And, although people today do not usually recognize it, God does not answer those prayer requests with sometimes *yes*, and sometimes *no*, and sometimes *maybe* or *wait a while*. All of the covenant promises in him are Yea, and in him amen. *(II Corinthians 1:20)*

Any failure of fulfilled prayer requests totally finds its basis in doubt and unbelief *(Matthew 17:20; Mark 11:24)* or in asking amiss. *(James 4:3)* It is not because God is not pleased with us; or that we have not been a good boy or good girl this week, or that God has so many other things to do that He does not have any time for me right now; or any other flaky notions that Scripturally uninformed men and women would presume to come up with in an attempt to take the spotlight off of their neglected responsibilities and place the blame, or failure of receiving, on God. God does His job, the Angels do their job, and we need to recognize, and then do our job.

#9. ***"In the year that king Uzziah died I saw also the Lord sitting upon a throne, high and lifted up, and his train filled the temple.***

Above it stood the seraphims: each one has six wings; with twain he covered his face, and with twain he covered his feet, and with twain he did fly.

And one cried unto another, and said, Holy, holy, holy, is the Lord of host: the whole earth is full of his glory." *(Isaiah 6:1-3)*

The Israeli prophet Isaiah was blessed at a given point in time to receive a vision from the Lord. His physical eyes were opened unto the invisible realm, and he gazed upon the Lord Himself, sitting upon His throne.

In attendance to the Lord, at the time, were mature male, angelic beings holding the rank of Seraph. Their duty was to utter declarations of adoration and pronouncements of holiness. Actual worship is what is being witnessed, and it would seem, that even as the Cherubim are assigned the responsibility of guardianship, at various times and in various places; so the Seraphim are assigned the delights of worship and adoration. Is this a 24/7 assignment activity for these Seraphs? Are these particular Angels not involved in any other type of activity? Have they no social life?

In addition to Cherubs, and Seraphs, there are various other ranks of angelic beings. Watchers *(Daniel 4:13-23)* and generic Sons of God . . . both holy and unholy. *(Genesis 6:2 & 4; Job 1:6; 2:1; 38:7)* Living Creatures *(Ezekiel 10:15 & 17 & 20)* *[although the name of Cherubim is within these verses, these creatures have four wings, and four faces, and four hands . . . the guardian Cherubim within the tabernacle of the congregation, in the Holy of Holies, do not. Nor do the cherubim stationed outside of the eastern gate to the Garden of Eden]* and Beasts *(Revelation 4:6-9; 5:6; 11; 14; 6:1; 3; 5; 7)* and the Archangel. *(I Thessalonians 4:16; Jude 9)*

#10. "But the prince of the kingdom of Persia withstood me one and twenty days: but, lo, Michael, one of the chief princes, came to help me; and I remained there with the kings of Persia.

Now I am come to make thee understand what shall befall thy people in the latter days: for yet the vision is for many days.

And when he had spoken such words unto me, I set my face toward the ground, and I became dumb.

And, behold, one like the similitude of the sons of men touched my lips: then I opened my mouth, and spake, and said unto him that stood before me, O my lord, by the vision my sorrows are turned upon me, and I have retained no strength.

For how can the servant of this my lord talk with this my lord? for as for me, straightway there remained no strength in me neither is there breath left in me.

Then there came again and touched me one like the appearance of a man, and he strengthened me,

And said, O man greatly beloved, fear not: peace be unto thee, be strong, yea, be strong. And when he had spoken unto me, I was strengthened, and said, Let my lord speak; for thou hast strengthened me.

> *Then said he, Knowest thou wherefore I come unto thee? and now will I return to fight with the prince of Persia: and when I am gone forth, lo, the prince of Grecia shall come.*
>
> *But I will shew thee that which is noted in the scripture of truth: and there is none that holdeth with me in these things, but Michael your prince."* (Daniel 10:13-21)

The Book of Daniel is looked upon by many as being the Revelation of the Old Testament. This particular incident shows us the Holy Angel Gabriel's dilemma, of angelic contestation.

The unholy, Fallen Angel of influence, over the earthly kingdom of Persia, has stopped Gabriel cold in his tracks. And Gabriel is unable to defeat him and is delayed twenty-one days, *(Daniel 10:13)* in his assignment. Whereupon, one of the holy, chief angelic princes, named Michael, comes to his aid, and frees him to continue on in his assignment, to bring the answer to Daniel's prayer request. *(Daniel 9:4)*

An unknown Holy Angel personally ministers to Daniel, and physically strengthens him *(Daniel 10:18)* in the midst of this unseen contestation turmoil.

Conflict occurs between the unholy angelic prince of the kingdom of Persia, and the Holy Angel Gabriel.

Conflict also occurs between the holy angelic prince named Michael and the unholy angelic prince of the kingdom of Persia.

And future conflict is foretold between the Holy Angel named Gabriel, and the unholy angelic prince of the kingdom of Persia; with the result being that the unholy angelic prince of the kingdom of Persia shall be deposed, and the unholy angelic prince of the kingdom of Grecia shall take his place. *(Daniel 10:20)* There is an assumption that when he returns, Gabriel shall be aided by Michael in obtaining his victory since Gabriel was not able to prevail against the unholy angelic prince of the kingdom of Persia by himself.

What we are able to observe here, is the reality that Angels personally minister to covenant individuals, and that Angels actually engage in, if you will, hand to hand combat.

#11. ***"Take heed that ye despise not one of these little ones; for I say unto you, That in heaven their angels do always behold the face of my Father which is in heaven."*** *(Matthew 18:10)*

This is a Scripture verse that has contributed to the idea of *Guardian Angels*, particularly where little children are concerned. It is an accepted belief that every person on Earth has a *Guardian Angel*, whose job it is to protect them from harm and to watch our over them. There is no Scripture passage to confirm this notion, but still, it remains an established belief axiom within humanity.

What is so, is that any individual that is in a blood covenant relationship with the living God is afforded angelic assistance, in a myriad of administrative manners. Any individual that is not in a blood covenant relationship with the living God has no legal standing before the God of grace, and as such, God is not in any way legally obligated to that person; either to protect them, or to provide for them, or to guide them in the affairs of this life.

#12. ***"He saw in a vision evidently about the ninth hour of the day an angel of God coming in to him, and saying unto him, Cornelius.***
And when he looked on him, he was afraid, and said, What is it Lord? And he said unto him, Thy prayers and thine alms are come up for a memorial before God." *(Acts 10:2-3)*

Angels guide individual persons to gospel workers. However, what we should glean from this incident, and what needs to be understood, is that Cornelius was a man inclined unto the things of eternal value in the first place. He was not just some guy, wandering around on the street, who could really care less about eternal issues. He was interested, concerning the things of the living God. *(Hebrews 11:6)*

And so it will be with any person, no matter where they are located on this planet, whose heart is honestly seeking after truth, and who yearns for the knowledge of the One True God. Those persons will have the hand of God extended unto them many times using the ministry of Angels. And since God is not willing that any should perish, *(II Peter 3:9)* He will seize every opportunity that presents itself.

#13. *"But while he thought on these things, behold, the angel of the Lord appeared unto him in a dream, saying, Joseph, thou son of David, fear not to take unto thee Mary thy wife: for that which is conceived in her is of the Holy Ghost." (Matthew 1:20)*

Then Joseph being raised from sleep did as the angel of the Lord had bidden him, and took unto him his wife:" *(Matthew 1: 24)*

Within humanity, for many people, a dream is a very, very real occurrence; and yet, at the same time, it is not. There is not a lot of information concerning the *Dream-World* that most people enjoy. Fantasy fulfillment, supernatural abilities realized, victorious confrontations, as well as fearful anxiety, dashing of hopes, and situations of terror. A proposed definition of a dream emanating forth from the *Dream-World* would be: *a product from the activity of the human mind, in an unconscious state, manifesting data input from the five physical senses; without the assurance of whether it will be good or bad. It is the end product of what you are not really aware of, that you are focusing on.*

Incredibly, and as hard as it may be to understand how it is done, Angels are able to interface with this unconscious mental activity. Consider please, that one of the reasons for the allowance of this is that Satan, the regent of the kingdom of darkness, is not able to read the Human mind. And it is through this interfacing that God, at key points in time, has successfully given instruction to responsible individuals, to which the kingdom of darkness was not ever privy.

The very fact that it can, and has, happened, should give us an indication of what may be out there concerning an unseen realm of reality that sooner or later, we are going to come to know the intricacies and nuances of.

#14. *"For the Son of man shall come in the glory of his Father with his angels; and then he shall reward every man according to his works."* (Matthew 16:27)

"When the Son of man shall come in his glory, and all the holy angels with him, then shall he sit upon the throne of his glory." (Matthew 25:31)

There are two separate events that these two Scriptures refer to. The first Scripture verse, and the first event that goes with it, is the fulfillment of that mystery *(I Corinthians 15:51)* that we now know of, as the Rapture of the Church. Holy Angels, carrying the spirit/soul compliments of the saints of God, shall return from the Father's house to the planet Earth, in order that those very saints might receive their glorified Spiritual bodies.

The second Scripture verse, and the second event that goes with it, is the actual Second Coming of Christ to the Earth, to deal with the Antichrist, the False Prophet, Satan, and the supportive Human constituency of rebellion.

Holy angels assist in many of the aspects of the Plan of Redemption for Mankind. They accompany the New Creation Christ Jesus in his return to the Earth, to assist and accomplish the bidding of Jesus.

#15. *"And there was war in heaven: Michael and his angels fought against the dragon; and the dragon fought and his angels,*

And prevailed not; neither was their place found any more in heaven.

And the great dragon was cast out, that old serpent, called the Devil, and Satan, which deceiveth the whole world: he was cast out into the earth, and his angels were cast out with him." (Revelation 12:7-9)

Within the Book of Daniel, we observed conflict between the Holy Angels of Gabriel and Michael, and the unholy angelic princes of the kingdoms of Persia and Grecia; but it was only conflict, and not all out war. There was influential, kingdom oversight-transition taking place, which brought about an actual kingdom fall-and-rise change, concerning the nations and the people on the Earth.

However, within the Book of Revelation situation, we have reached the point of imposed probational-time-constraints. We are witnessing Satan's complete eviction, and casting down from the atmospheric first heaven of planet Earth, and the expelling of all of his angelic company toadies as well. This occurs as a result of angelic warfare. Hand to hand combat, if you will, between Holy and unholy Angels. And, since one cannot kill an Angel, we are actually looking at positional advantage or disadvantage, and the surety of securing that advantage. By Divine decree, just as the waves of the sea have their instructions concerning their operating boundaries, *(Psalm 104:9)* so Satan and his angelic forces are not allowed to ascend from the Earth up into the heaven ever again.

#16. *"And I saw an angel come down from heaven, having the key to the bottomless pit and a great chain in his hand.*
And he laid hold on the dragon, that old serpent, which is the Devil, and Satan, and bound him a thousand years,
And cast him into the bottomless pit, and shut him up, and set a seal upon him, that he should deceive the nations no more, till the thousand years should be fulfilled: and after that he must be loosed a little season." *(Revelation 20:1-3)*

Our last example of angelic activity involves the extended temporary incarceration of Satan, and the action of him being bound with a great chain, for a one thousand year period of time. It is usually preached that Michael is the Angel that will execute this particular task; however, there is no mention of that being the case, anywhere within the Scriptures.

What we do have, is the reality of an incident of a Holy Angel incapacitating and jailing an unholy angel. This is the kind of activity that we would be able to associate with Human Beings without any difficulty, because of what we are familiar with on this Earth. However, for that to be happening within the angelic realm without some sort of societal parameters, would seem to be a bit odd.

In summation, we can see, just within these sixteen Scriptural examples, that Angels are quite active within normal societal parameters. And, there is even more that they can do, within their capacity as ministers of God:

As a review, they can bring answers to prayer *(Daniel 9:21-23; Acts 10)* and impart the will of God. *(Acts 5:19-20)* They can convey revelations *(II Kings 1:15; Daniel 8:19)* and guard the Tree of Life. *(Genesis 3:24)* They can receive the departed spirits of men *(Luke 16:22)* and convey certain laws. *(Acts 7:53)* They can witness the confessions of men *(Luke 15:8-9)* and will accompany Christ Jesus to the Earth when he returns. *(Matthew 25:31; II Thessalonians 1:7-10)* When it is time, they will separate the good from the bad *(Matthew 13:39-41)* and will protect individuals that are in a blood covenant relationship with God. *(Psalm 34:7; 91:11; Acts 12:7-10)* They will re-gather the Nation of Israel when it is time *(Matthew 24:31)* and they will unlock a specific gate at a specific point in time. *(Revelation 9:1)* They minister before the Lord God Almighty *(Revelation 8:2; 14:15-19)* and will bind Satan with a strong chain, when the time comes. They appear to men in their dreams to give them guidance *(Matthew 1:20-24)* and they direct gospel preachers in their commission. *(Acts 8:26; 27:23)* They lead sinners to encounter gospel workers *(Acts 10:3)* and will strengthen individuals who are in a trial. *(Matthew 4:11; Luke 22:43)* They will sing, and praise, and worship God *(Luke 2:13; Psalm 103:20; 148:2)* and will minister to and help each individual. *(Matthew 18:10)* They influentially rule over the various nations of the Earth, from the unseen realm *(Daniel 10:13-21)* and are used by God to execute lawful judgments. *(Genesis 19; II Samuel 24; Psalm 78:49; Revelation 15:1-16:2)* In actual combat with one another, they wage war *(Revelation 12:7-9)* and they drive spirit horse-drawn chariots. *(II Kings 2:12; 6:13-17; Zechariah 1:7-11)* Angels are also the scribes of heaven. God has prepared two specific written accounts: the first one, is the Book of Life *(Revelation 13:8)* for those who have placed their eternal trust in the finished work of the Lord Jesus Christ. The second account, are the *books* that have been prepared to record all errant activities of thought, word, and deed, from every disobedient, rebellious, spiritual criminal that exists. *(Revelation 20:12)* Someone has to record all of those names, or sadly, blot them out, of the combined works. God has appointed certain angels to accomplish that particular task.

Holy Angelic Society interfaces and intertwines with Human Society, because of Sin, rebellion, desired redemption, and probational personal decisions, from the Express Image of his Person creatures *(Genesis 1:26; Hebrews 1:3)* that teeter on the precarious fulcrum of free-will.

There may have been angelic interaction with the previous Social Order that existed on this Earth, prior to the creation of Adam and Eve, but that interaction would be substantially different from what we are able to see Scripturally because the whole constituency of the Angels themselves, were still in the midst of their own probational decisions.

FOUR

Where is it That Angels Live?

Normally, the average person does not give much thought to the idea that angels live anywhere at all, do they? Is it not pretty much believed that the average angel just flies around, all over the place, and at certain junctures in time, goes and does what God tells them to do?

Since, in other areas of life that we are familiar with, it does not actually work that way, there might be more to the life activities of angels than we normally understand.

A very good question to ask ourselves when we begin to give thought to the actual residency of angels is: Where is it that God Himself lives? He is a real person, is He not, and He must dwell somewhere. Or, is it the case that God and His throne *(Revelation 3:21)* and His garden *(Ezekiel 28:13)* and the other amenities that He has, are just floating around somewhere in outer-space, with no place to be able to call *home*. And, when we consider that ridiculous concept, there are just a few Scriptural notations that we might want to give some recognition and thought to.

"For he looked for a city which hath foundations, whose builder and maker *is* God." *(Hebrews 11:10)*
"And I John saw the holy city, new Jerusalem, coming down from God out of heaven, prepared as a bride adorned for her husband." *(Revelation 21:2)*

These two verses alone, testify to us of the reality of a genuine city, that many men refer to as the City of God.

Now, we know that cities do not normally just float around in the atmospheric air of this planet, or even float around out in the outer space regions of this universe, but rather that they must have their very foundations set upon real solid ground.

The cities that the creatures called Men have built are established and secured only on this planet that we call Earth. The cities that God has had built are established and secured on the planet that Scripture calls Heaven *(II Corinthians 12:2-4). Normally speaking, Heaven is another of a myriad of Scriptural subjects that are not intelligently talked about, because of a lack of knowledge (Hosea 4:6).* Nevertheless, the planet of Heaven is a real place, with real cities built upon it, and real objects and furniture situated within those cities, and real inhabitants occupying those cities, involved with real activities of life. And, the New Jerusalem is just one of potentially how many cities that may be built on that planet called Heaven?

Where do aborted babies go? Where do still-born children go? Where do Human Beings that die in infancy go? Where do young children, who have not reached the age-of-accountability, and are inadvertently killed go? To be sure, they **do not** go . . . *out of existence*. There is no valid Scriptural doctrine anywhere, for any free will moral creature, to ever go *out of existence*, once they have been created or, within Humanity, conceived. So, where do they go? And please understand that, Jewish-Jesus of Nazareth's statement concerning

"You must be born-again" in order to enter into the Kingdom of God, is not a joke or a suggestion, but rather is a mandatory requirement of every individual on planet Earth, and should not be taken lightly *(John 3:3; 5).*

Although the New Jerusalem is the only city upon the planet Heaven that we know the specific name of, to have any inhabited planet with only one single city located on it, is ludicrous, to say the least. And, considering that the city of New Jerusalem is 1,500 miles wide, and 1,500 miles deep, and 1,500 miles high *(Revelation 21:16)*, the planet itself that the city is currently located on, must be substantially larger than planet Earth to be able to accommodate the larger cities that are potentially located thereon.

It is believed by some, and this author is one of those that believe, that conceived Human Beings, under covenant protection *(I Corinthians 7:14)*, will find themselves within one of the numerous unnamed cities on the planet Heaven, where they will be raised up unto maturity by angelic overseers and tutors. And that, at some point in time, they will each be challenged to place their trust in the finished work of New Creation Jesus of Nazareth, and pass from spiritual-death unto spiritual-life *(John 3:3; 5; I John 3:14)*.

This author is also persuaded that angels are the skilled craftsmen of every vocation that built all of these different cities; and that the angels are also potentially the ones who are in charge of the raising up of these candidates for receptivity to everlasting life and universal reign. *[Please remember that the angel Lucifer was once in a position of governance and oversight, concerning a mature, lower form of creation]*

The planet of Heaven itself, is certainly large enough to accommodate, and house, the unnumbered multitude of angelic beings that have been designed to serve God; and now that Mankind is on the scene, to serve him as well *(Hebrews 1:14)*.

We know that the city of New Jerusalem is the city that was built by God *(Hebrews 11:10)*, possibly utilizing angelic craftsmen, and that it is referred to by Jewish-Jesus of Nazareth as "my Father's house" *(John 14:2)*. We also know from Scriptural records that there are opulent mansions there within the city, awaiting the arrival and occupation of the children of the Most High God *(John 14:2)*. This author is also persuaded that the same skilled, vocational angelic craftsmen that built both the city of New Jerusalem, and the unnamed cities on the planet Heaven, also custom build, to personal taste, the opulent mansions that God will delight in presenting to each of His children as a gift. And in the process, angelic craftsmen would be responsible for constructing any of their own residences as well, that may be within that same city of the New Jerusalem.

In light of these issues, it is proposed that angels actually have an active social order, operating and inter-twined, within the affairs and activities that occur upon this Earth, as well as within the city of the New Jerusalem specifically. And even more pronounced, that they are active and operating within the various unnamed cities that will forever remain upon the planet Heaven.

In breaking down the same 24-hour repetitive time cycle that God has established concerning Mankind, and that is operating at least for this particular solar-system; we have times of eating, times of sleeping, times of personal hygiene, times of sexual activity, times of required labor, time for leisure activities, and times of focused worship of the One True God. Might the angelic social order run along similar guidelines? Might they have times of eating, or does the Celestial Body not need to be sustained in any manner? Might they have times of sleeping, or does the Celestial Body not need a period of regeneration in any aspect? Might they have times of personal hygiene, or are Celestial Bodies exempt from odor and filth? Angelic sexual activity is non-existent amongst the Holy Angels, primarily due to the fact that there are no female angelic compliments. And, it would seem, angelic procreation was not originally a Divinely designed activity. Required labor does seem to be substantiated by the various notations that we have within the Scriptures with regards to what angels do, but is there no leisure time afforded? Are they only *Energizer Bunny* creatures that have no allotted time of respite, simply continuous duty? Good questions all. And, last but not least, they definitely do have times of focused worship of the One True God *(Isaiah 6:1-3)*.

Now, specifically speaking, concerning the City of God, the New Jerusalem: as we speak, the city is currently, firmly attached to the planet named Heaven. However, in approximately 1,000 years from today, that will not be the case. At some point in time, the city is due to become detached from the planet Heaven, and relocated to a position just above the atmosphere of this planet Earth. *This possibly might be only a one-time occurrence, for the purpose of close physical harmony and operation, between the Universal Corporate Headquarters for Administration, Maintenance, and Governance. And the Universal Corporate Headquarters for the Colonization of Mankind.*

Just how God is going to do this phenomenal feat is not known; nevertheless, it will indeed happen *(Matthew 19:26; Revelation 21:2)*. For those who might think that this is physically or naturally not a plausible consideration, we would do well to remember Cloud City from the epic film *Star Wars Episode V*. Although there was no explanation as to how it was accomplished, nevertheless, the city hung suspended within the atmosphere of the planet, and was only able to be accessed by flight. And, although that is currently a product of science fiction, and a postulation out of the mind of a man, it will become a manifest reality for the city of New Jerusalem, at the end of Probation for Mankind that is currently in process.

Truly, angels are a marvelous creation. We normally are only familiar with Human Beings, and the various occurrences that swirl around within human society. We do hear about angels. We do see pictures of angels. We dream of flying around without the aid of any machine, just like angels can do. And we dream of doing supernatural exploits, and demonstrating prowess, just like we hear that angels are able to do. But sadly, too many times we really do not know very much more than that, concerning an unnumbered constituency of glorious beings who have been gifted with just as much *physical* life as we have.

Since the word of our God tells us, **"the things which are seen were not made of things which do appear,"** *(Hebrews 11:3)* and **"the invisible things of him from the creation of the world are clearly seen, being understood by the things that are made"** *(Romans 1:20)* we might do well to consider some of the things that we have just looked at.

This author believes that angels are social creatures and that God has designed them to interact with other social creatures. It is only reasonable to consider that angels have their own societal parameters that they actively operate within. May we consider to what extent that might be the case, and trust the Lord for the remainder.

The blessing of the Lord be upon thee. Maranatha!

Meet the Author

By-The-Book Ministries, Inc. began in 2001 as a teaching outreach. Rob E. Daley has been gifted by God to be able to explain biblical truths in an easy to understand manner.

Many have been blessed by his teaching style.

Rob was saved and filled with the Holy Spirit in 1978 and has been instructed by the greatest teacher of all—the Spirit of Truth Himself. Rob is an ordained minister with the Assemblies of God International Fellowship and has pastored in various churches over the past 34 years.

It is the desire of this ministry to see the body of Christ solidly taught, and grow up into the things of the Lord. Rob is available for seminars, retreats, conventions, etc.

Rob can be reached at:

thedaleys@bythebookministries.org

http://robdaleyauthor.com

About the Cover

The cover image is titled "Moon Set over Earth" and was taken from Space Shuttle Discovery during STS-70 mission.

NASA is not connected with nor do they endorse this book in any way.

www.ingramcontent.com/pod-product-compliance
Lightning Source LLC
Chambersburg PA
CBHW072022060426
42449CB00034B/1657